The Humanistic Teacher

For my very good friend,

Love,

Jerry

THE HUMANISTIC TEACHER

First the Child, Then Curriculum

*Jerome S. Allender and
Donna Sclarow Allender*

Paradigm Publishers
Boulder • London

Published in the United States by Paradigm Publishers, 3360 Mitchell Lane, Suite E, Boulder, CO 80301 USA.

Paradigm Publishers is the trade name of Birkenkamp & Company, LLC, Dean Birkenkamp, President and Publisher.

Library of Congress Cataloging-in-Publication Data
Allender, Jerome S.
    The humanistic teacher : first the child, then curriculum / Jerome S. Allender and Donna Sclarow Allender.
        p. cm.
    Includes bibliographical references and index.
    ISBN-13: 978-1-59451-524-8 (hardcover : alk. paper)
    1. Education, Humanistic.   2. Teachers—In-service training.   I. Allender, Donna Sclarow.   II. Title.
    LC1011.A548 2008
    371.11'2—dc22
                                        2007052275

Printed and bound in the United States of America on acid free paper that meets the standards of the American National Standard for Permanence of Paper for Printed Library Materials.

Designed and Typeset by Mulberry Tree Enterprises.

12   11   10   09   08   1   2   3   4   5

*To Abe and Bessie Sclarow and Frank and Ede Allender.
Especially to Ede who, after raising four children,
with only a fifth-grade education, went back to school
and on to achieving a master's degree in education from
the University of Chicago. She was a wonderful
humanistic teacher until she was 85. Though she
learned many of her skills from us, she was the model.
We are thankful for the gifts of our parents.*

Contents

Prologue

We present a collage of ideas constructed out of pieces of history, personal experiences, theory, and mostly successful practices to demonstrate the possibility of becoming a humanistic teacher. For all the problems that are faced in the classroom, in the reality we see, there is hope. Not a utopia by a long shot, yet there are ways of thinking, feeling, and acting that are within reach—in any school.

What is a humanistic teacher? Simply, the answer is a teacher who considers the needs of a student before the requirements of the curriculum. This means the teacher is trusted to negotiate with students and parents how the curriculum will be sometimes expanded, sometimes contracted, and taught. All together, they work out the needs of the student. Though the design remains mainly the responsibility of teachers, this critical process creates an especially effective, collaborative educational environment. The teachers who have been our students have been encouraged to draw on our ideas and mix them with their own—as they figured out personal preferences. In effect, they experienced a curriculum where their needs were being met. This course of study enabled them to weave together ideas, hopes, and personal strengths. We encourage readers to spend the time it takes to reflect on the collage we create by the chapters ahead and form the definition of the teacher they want to become. First and foremost, we are concerned with the practical. The case study that is discussed in the first two chapters is about a humanistic school. Here, we are able to see examples of successful practices most plainly. From this vantage, we then have to build theories and ask how they play out in circumstances that are more difficult. We keep in mind an education that truly serves student needs, never losing sight of meeting the needs of the teacher too. In Part Three, we tell stories of teachers and schools in faraway lands that help us to dispel assumptions of what can't be possible. We go on to explore new methods of research that respond to the concerns of the practitioner and serve as models for teachers who might undertake their own educational inquiries. In the last chapter, we share ideas and experiences that touch on what an individual teacher can attempt and hope for. Throughout, we write letters to our grandson, Dylan, who is five years old at this writing. They are meant to convey our stories.

- What was your education like? Think about the ways you want to teach the same as or differently than you were taught.
- Before turning to the first couple of chapters, pose a few questions you would like answered.
- Regularly, mark in your mind, on paper, or in the book, if you find an idea you believe would work for you.
- Keep in mind that you are developing your own definition of the good teacher—what we are likely to see as a humanistic teacher.

Acknowledgments

We appreciate the thoughts and ideas that family and colleagues have shared with us. Special thanks go to our daughters, Rachel Allender and Simone Allender, and our colleagues, Ed Kiess, Stefinee Pinnegar, Mary Lynn Hamilton, Robert Bullough, Donald Blumenfeld-Jones, Liz Schlesinger, Fran Fox, Nancy Bailey, Lisa Pack, Lucy Miller, and Tom Russell. Our publisher, Dean Birkenkamp, encouraged us, and together with Beth Davis, our editor, provided ongoing support and challenged us to write the book we wanted to write.

1

A Case Study

The most prominent worry that teachers and parents have about a humanistic educational program concerns the potential chaos that might result from this kind of school. We present a brief study of Project Learn (PL)—where Donna taught for more than twenty years and after retiring continues to help—to demonstrate how the program works on a daily basis. Chaos is not part of the picture. What is salient is a detailed structure that serves to guide the teachers and students in their work together, just as it serves to encourage and guide the regular contributions of the parents.

As an interactive community, there is a high degree of democratic participation. An important aspect is to create a sense of freedom to learn—with the explicit understanding that there are significant responsibilities that must be carried out by everyone. Though most teachers and parents have come from experiences in more traditional schools, there are many who offer special skills to the overall functioning of the program. No different than anywhere else, the program is designed to meet a multitude of needs. In the case of Project Learn, however, the highest priority is to meet the needs of the students as they are determined in discussions that involve teachers, students, and parents, sometimes in pairs, and at times all together. There is no doubt that the teachers are in charge, at the request of the parents and for the needs of the teachers, but just so, it is each student's needs that are most often given the higher priority. What marks the character of the school, in addition to the specifics of what will be learned, is the variety of opportunities that open up for the students as well as the staff and the parents.

Chapters 1 and 2 tell a story in detail of how the Project Learn community carries out its philosophy in practical terms.

- Pay attention to when your curiosity is aroused. Make a couple of notes about what you are looking for in the next chapters.
- Notice your concerns and, possibly, skepticism. Put them aside temporarily in an effort to gain a more complete understanding of the story as a whole. (Don't worry, you won't forget them if they are important.)
- Ask what you believe creates an educational environment that makes a teacher safe, in all senses, in the classroom.
- Then, wonder about how this safety contributes to a willingness to accept challenge and risks as a teacher.

1

Project Learn:
A Humanistic School

A poster hangs in Jerry's study with a quote from Reinhold Niebuhr: "We should be far less concerned with the purity of our actions and much more concerned with the integrity of our compromises." It is a philosophical position that makes idealism practical. The sentiment stands as one of the guiding principles for the staff, students, and parents of the Project Learn School.

THE BEGINNING

Imagine you are a student in a class intent on teaching you about humanistic education. You may be a preservice teacher hoping to be one of the best teachers ever, a parent looking to find a more lively school for your child, or a seasoned teacher wanting to reconnect with the idealism that brought you into teaching. We start this class with the story of a humanistic school in Philadelphia. Though few of you have ever seen such a school, it is important for all of us to know what is possible. Many of the educational environments with which we live are restrictive and discouraging, demanding that we teach in ways we swore we would never teach. The culture of testing undermines our sense of ourselves as teachers and parents, for we participate in the judging of our children by standards set by folks who do not know our children.

Perhaps what is most important for us in this class is what we can learn from the struggles of the people who tried to fully express their ideals. Though they were often very successful in the early years of the school, they too have had to deal with the pressures that today constrict educational environments everywhere.

It is our intention that each of us is able to use those elements of Project Learn that trigger our own internal idealism and stimulate our sense of how in our own schools we can, with a mischievous twinkle in our eye, implement maybe just a bit more of what we would like to see happen. The school was started in 1970 when the climate for change was open to ideals. It weathered many attempts to limit its program and as you will see in Chapter 10 has succumbed to some external pressures. Folks there still struggle to figure out how to balance the expression of their core beliefs with the world as it is now. The school is not the perfect model of its stated values, but it is good enough. And we encourage you to appreciate your own efforts to humanize your classes, schools, or wherever you engage with children, even if they are not perfect. Believe that what you do when you intend to place the needs of your children first when planning your curriculum will be good enough.

A LETTER FOR DYLAN FROM DONNA

We wonder what you think about this letter written to our grandson, not yet in kindergarten, for him to read someday when he is older. It's for him to ponder about how Project Learn began.

Dear Dylan,

Your mother, Rachel, was an ideal kindergarten student. She loved school, loved her teacher, cleaned the brushes after painting, sat in circle and listened attentively to other children, and talked excitedly to Grangran and me each day about what happened. I volunteered one day a week in her classroom and was the substitute teacher when her teacher was unable to be there. All was well with public education. When your mother went to first grade everything changed. She was in seats in rows rather than at tables, and she had to sit still most of the day. It wasn't so hard to get her to go to school each morning, but I nearly had to drag her there after lunch. She just didn't want to go back. One day I asked why, and she said the most interesting thing. "School doesn't make sense. I wanted to learn the word 'yellow' today but the teacher said that I had to learn 'red.' I didn't want to learn 'red.'" She had a very good reason to learn yellow. Her best friend had trouble saying that word, and she wanted to be able to teach her how to read it.

After a week or so of this sad, difficult time, I went to the teacher to discuss what was going on for Rachel and how your grandfather and I could be helpful to her. The teacher said something that changed me forever. "Don't worry, Mrs. Allender. She'll get used to it." I responded, "Yes, you are absolutely right. She will get used to it. We all got used to it." And, Dylan, dear, it was at that moment that I was clear that this was not the way Rachel would be educated. Fortunately, an alternative, humanistic program was being formed in an empty North Philadelphia school building. We signed Rachel up to be one of the students at the Paxson Parkway Public School. Within a month I became one of the teachers (with an agreement that your Aunt Simone who was then two and a half years old could attend unofficially), and within four months we were closed by the School District for political reasons. But the parents decided to continue the program on their own, and we called the new school, Project Learn, which means Living Experiences About Reality Now. Soon, we just called ourselves PL.

After a few years of being an illegal school waiting to return to the public school system, we received a letter from the state of Pennsylvania's Department of Education. It told us that they knew we existed and that we were not legal. It said we should not involve the state in the politics of Philadelphia and for us to just apply for a license as a private school. This was not an easy thing for the members of the PL community. We were all public school people and had no intention of running a private school. There were long discussions and the final Town Meeting, where the parents decided to apply for the license, ran until 3:00 a.m. Almost every parent stayed until the decision was made. We chose to become legal because we ultimately cared more about the education of our children than about our politics.

Very soon after sending in the license application, we received notice that a state inspector was coming out to evaluate whether we were worthy of being a licensed private school. We were told that the gentleman was an experienced inspector and a person who had taught high school Latin for twenty-five years. Everyone at PL was really nervous about this man coming to evaluate our program. We knew he would be really critical of how children had choices about what they did and how limited our physical resources were. So we gathered together some of the folks in our community, sure to include our three Ph.D.'s, to be at the meeting with him after school. We hoped to impress him with how academic we were.

The day came and he came. He spent the whole day moving between the different groups of children. At the end of the day, we all gathered in a circle in the little mismatched chairs we had. I introduced him to all the parents and then he started to talk. Well, Dylan, all of us to the person were shocked by what he said. He told us that this was the very best school he had ever evaluated. He said he wished all children could have the kind of education we were providing for ours. Most schools were much better looking and had many more things, but not one of them had the kind of human resources we were providing. It was clear to him that our children were really learning what they needed to know. The one complaint he had, with a smile on his face, was that he knew he would never have to come to the school again to check up on the areas that didn't pass licensing, because he said that we would get a full license just as we were.

PL was housed in several church basements and rented spaces, but after three years, we bought an old pill factory on Germantown Avenue and made it our home. By this time, the staff included the three women who would become known as the founding mothers: Fran Fox, Nancy Bailey, and myself. All of us had been teachers elsewhere. On the day the building became ours, the three of us walked in with our eight children to clean and make it ready to be a school. As we worked, the children explored and within a very short time, the first permanent rule of Project Learn was made. Children may never slide down the banisters or they will be sent home. You can be sure that many of the students took serious issue with that rule and more than once tried to get it overturned in a town meeting but to no avail. It stands to this day along with two other nonnegotiable rules: A child who bites another child will be sent home. There will be no kinds of guns in the school. Though I felt strongly about this third rule, it was Fran who was adamant about it. Children were not permitted to even put their fingers out and say "bang, bang" when she was on yard duty. And the rest of us were careful not to allow it, because we knew someone would tell Fran, and we would get in trouble with her.

There are a few more rules that developed over the years. One of them is that any child may join a group game in the backyard. No one may be excluded. We also have the policy that fights are settled by the fighters sitting down and talking. One day I was on yard duty and a big disagreement occurred—a fight really—about who would be on which team. Fran's son Dan was in the game, and I heard him yell to the rest of the kids, "Stop, we have to figure this out ourselves or Donna will stop the game and make us talk, and we'll use up all of our recess talking." Or as another student was once heard to say, "We'll be sentenced to death!"

The stories about PL seem endless. Many make me laugh and some make me cry, with a smile. I hope you too will have a lot of laughing, and I'm sure there will be a few tears in your years at Project Learn.

Love, Nana

A SCHOOL COMMUNITY

"Project Learn: A School Community" is how the sign reads hanging to the side of the main entrance. The Paxson Parkway Elementary School, an amalgam of teachers and students from Philadelphia's inner city and the more affluent Mt. Airy community about a twenty-minute drive apart, closed in December after only four months, not even making it to the end of a regular semester. As a public alternative school, it was part of a larger innovative effort by the Philadelphia Public School District to offer students opportunities to enroll in unusual humanistic programs, with a primary focus on the high school years. Paxson Parkway was its only elementary school, and in this case, complaints were raised about how the racial balance in one of the feeder schools had been seriously undermined. It happened that too many white children had agreed to travel to the inner city to attend. It was a reasonable complaint. But for the parents, the teachers, and the children who had enrolled in this new school, the closing was a problem. They had finally found a program that met their needs. The vision of the teachers and the hopes of the parents were too close to being realized to let go of it. A small group of these energetic, idealistic parents, about thirty-five families depending on when they were counted, decided that they wanted to keep the school open.

In an early discussion, the group recognized that only by charging a minimal tuition would many of the students be able to continue. Karolyn Snyder and Donna agreed to work for low salaries to make it possible. Karolyn's fervor had led to the start of a small basement school in her home in Mt. Airy the year before. All of those students enrolled in Paxson when it opened, and she was hired as one of the teachers. For the new school, two assistant teachers were also hired, space was rented, time was invested, and classes began to meet mid-January. The school might have been bigger, but many who had attended for the first four months at Paxson were unwilling to leave the public school system. Each of us had to weigh where our integrity lay. Those who became the founders held on to the belief that, though initially we were an illegal school, we would be welcomed back someday soon. There was good evidence that the children were being educated among the best ways possible. But finally to avoid a showdown with the city and the state, it became necessary two years later to apply for a license. By then it was way too late for those who had continued with the school to give up what had been built. It was odd for both of us, having grown up in the Midwest where only the wealthy elite went to private schools. Now, it seemed that we were among them.

We consoled ourselves by believing that we had expanded the meaning of private school to alternative school.

Like nomads, the school moved from place to place during the first three years; we appreciated the gifts of many. At first, it was self-evident that the parents would all participate in the running of the school, because there was no one else to do it. A cleaning schedule was set up; some parents had responsibilities for teaching or assisting teachers and others for yard duty when the children went out to play. Outside community resources were a big part of the program, and transportation when needed was provided by carpools. Evening committee work came only after breathing, and often instead of eating meals in a normal fashion. A monthly "town meeting" was established where new ideas were explored, the functioning of old ones improved, and the final decisions were made. The buck stopped there.

Today, Project Learn stands in the Germantown area of Philadelphia, not the inner city, but maybe better—in a racially mixed community of people with a wide range of means. The tuition is higher in order to provide teachers with a salary that is a little closer to a living wage, though it does make difficulties for more people who might want their children to attend. And still, the cost is far less than other private schools. The building has been expanded to accommodate 100 students with more than ten paid teachers, when all the people who help out are included. Of the changes, two are particularly noteworthy and clearly for the good: no is likely to use the word chaos anymore, and added to the official name are the words, *A Parent Cooperative*. Still, from the cleaning schedule to the town meeting, the to-do list has stayed fairly close to what it was in the beginning. It is kind of amazing that the enthusiasm renews itself each succeeding year.

There are many reasons to account for the longevity of Project Learn. Like many alternative schools that were founded around this time, the driving impetus was to create a school that differed from the norm, in opposition to how children were generally being taught. Without more distinctive guiding principles, most of these schools have long since closed. The PL teachers and parents worked long hours, often too late into the evening, to craft an innovative educational theory reflecting many of the interests and concerns of the community as a whole—with a process that challenged the community to continue crafting the theory as part of the school's way of life.

But no less critical was a practical reality: the three teachers, Donna among them, along with Fran Fox and Nancy Bailey, who eventually became known as the founding mothers, or grandmothers as they now are. These three committed themselves to providing their own children with the kind of education that would fulfill a vision that grew out of idealism, compromise, and integrity. Only in the past ten years have these three finally retired, though each one of them continues to be involved. Today, they are succeeded by some of their relatives, children, and grandchildren as teachers and students. Furthermore, the new families who enroll their children, many from kindergarten through junior high, leave their own significant legacies that revitalize the program year after year. The plurality of visions causes trouble all the while that the multitudes of ideas contribute to the enthusiasm that gives the school new life. Of course, difficulties abound, but the evolving process like everything else has worked so far.

Then and now, there is no principal. But as the school grew in size, the concept of an educational coordinator developed. Someone was needed, not to make decisions about rules, policies, or principles, just someone to hold things together until long-standing decisions could be worked on. At first, this was a lead teacher who would make moment-to-moment decisions for the whole school. It was a kind of leadership that did not disenfranchise the leadership of individual members of the community. The hope persists that everyone will contribute to the vision that sustains the vitality of the program.

Neither memory nor records serve to remind us if the concept of checks and balances was in mind, but there is no question that in addition to a lead teacher—or whatever name was attached to the person who held the position over the years—there had to be a lead parent as well. Significantly, this included a responsibility to lead town meetings using consensus as the guiding principle—a difficult task. Every teacher had to keep this in mind when helping the children make decisions, and the teachers themselves had to practice what they preached in their meetings. But the biggest challenge was for the community at large. High aims like these can easily be frustrated by a lack of commitment to achieving consensus by members of the community, even one person. Without this commitment, the process can easily be undermined. For the PL community, a method for achieving a modified consensus worked best. There is a place for individuals to register their disagreement with a decision—without the intention of blocking the will of the group. And still, there is always the power of any one person to cast a blocking vote. The separation of the two helps people to better understand and be responsible for their actions in the town meeting.

We do remember how in the first year when things were not going at all smoothly, Donna walked out of school to "clear her thinking."

When she returned two days later, she put up a list of nonnegotiable demands, among them achieving consensus. Though it might seem paradoxical to some as a way of diminishing conflict in the present, she felt that achieving consensus had to be the foundation of the school's principles—along with no sliding down the banister, no biting, and no toy guns. Fundamentally, to make the school work, an equality of voice had to be given to everyone in the community. Around the same time, the community decided that every teacher, and the secretary, would be paid the same salary; raises when they materialized went to everyone equally. We grew to understand that a unity of purpose is what would connect the long- and short-term problems. It is fair to ask whether Donna was bluffing with her nonnegotiable demands. No one tested her. She doesn't know, so we'll never know.

The Project Learn community recognized that an equality of voice is a first priority, but as our grandson Dylan seems to know intuitively, there can be more than one first priority, however illogical that seems to Western-trained logical minds. Maintaining a building, particularly on a low budget, is another first. All the while that the problems of visionary leadership are confronted, someone has to be sure the toilets aren't overflowing. Nancy had a predilection for organizing the physical work that kept an old building safe and clean for all. Nobody called her a tyrant, but she had a way of seeing to it that the work got done. And, the name Parent Cooperative didn't deal with how the responsibility for doing this kind of work or any other was met. Fran became the community coordinator. She worked closely with the lead parent to make sure that everyone's share of cooperating was happening. Her leadership appeared in the form of a stubborn nag. As a part of their idealism, Donna's nonnegotiables, Nancy's tyranny, and Fran's determination became distinctive aspects of the school's personality for a long time—even when others took turns to assume these different leadership roles. And today, it's different, because of how little time the three of them spend at school. But as always, it is recognized that maintaining ideals requires strong leadership.

Back to the beginning: we remember how every member of the community was considered part of the consensus—including the children. Over the years, this ideal, taken from Neill's (1960) description of the Summerhill School, has eroded. In today's context, it doesn't seem like a significant loss. Right or wrong (which depends so much on context), children are no longer invited to cast a vote in the town meeting. In the early days, the rule was, if you could stay awake, your vote would be counted. It was not a perfect system. None is. But with tinkering from time to time, it has been working to keep the community's vision in focus and functioning.

The educational program was and is the other big first priority. Unlike Summerhill with its major focus on the politics of running the school, all would have been for naught if the children hadn't been provided with a humanistic educational environment, which was considered necessary to provide effective learning. Without benefit of titles, Nancy, Fran, and Donna divided up the full range of responsibilities, inviting and insisting on help from the staff, parents, and students to make up the whole. They appeared to be working for the most part as a dream team—in retrospect.

THE CURRICULUM

The Project Learn curriculum, as in other schools, is designed by educators but differently here. The design of the curriculum is the responsibility of the teachers who will do the teaching. Much of the work takes place in staff meetings. The opinions of others weigh in on the design with the tacit agreement that in the domain of teaching the teachers are first among equals. This status is achieved because of the time and effort put into the process: for doing their own homework; empowering discussions with students; considering parents' needs and concerns; planning lessons in detail, both alone and with team teachers; and attending outside seminars and courses relevant to subject and methods. Attention to expert research is also included in the mix, with special attention given to investigations that have been carried out in Project Learn's classrooms, often with the active participation of the teachers and the students, in ways that at times make everyone a co-researcher. It's more efficient to have a curriculum altogether handed down by experts, and help is appreciated, but to adequately address the needs of the students and the teachers takes more individual participation and meaningful choices. It is important to believe that teachers are capable of participating responsibly in the creation of their own teaching environment. It is this community belief that fosters a sense of agency for the teachers with, although no less important, secondary effects on the feelings of the students about their potential competence.

For all that the process of curriculum design is unusual, a first-time visitor entering Project Learn for a short while might see a school like many others. The basic subjects and materials are in many cases no different. Children are in classrooms, teachers are (usually) distinct from the students who are reading, writing, and doing arithmetic, or maybe drawing, painting, or playing music. Children's work is displayed on classroom walls and in the halls. Homework is mentioned regularly, and there are tests. Clearly, language arts, social studies, science, math, history, geography, and foreign language are being taught somewhere throughout the building. There are regular times when the students are playing in the schoolyard. Furthermore, even some of the humanistic characteristics appear at first to be within the range of normal expectations for a good school: children working in small groups, individual projects, and frequent discussions. Too, one will probably see conflicts being played out between students or students and teachers.

However, if the visitor pays just a little more attention, the humanistic characteristics of the program that distinguish it from other schools are apparent. No bells ring. Classrooms don't have doors. Children are moving around in the classroom and throughout the building, sometimes in small groups. Quite often, they don't ask permission, though they do inform their teacher where they are going. Students address teachers by their first names. There are no desks; there are tables to sit around. Chairs are often arranged in circles in an open space. In addition to adults helping individual children, students are helping one another. Sometimes, there is too much noise, yet most of the time the students are working. With all this commotion, the preponderance of on-task conversation is surprising for any elementary school.

More substantial observation is needed to appreciate the role of special courses; the impact of the variety requires a look over the years. There is a tradition at Project Learn to offer electives to students eight and older. Sometimes teachers simply offer them; other times they are requested by students; and at best, they are the result of planning discussions in which both take part. Some are limited by age, but others are offered to any student in the school, resulting in a wide spread of ages in the class. At the beginning of a semester, a list of offerings is handed out so that students can rank their choices. Alongside regular courses, opportunities arise for students to work on creative writing, remedial spelling, a literary journal, or the *P. L. Paper,* one of the longest running electives. Though art classes are a regular part of every child's studies, the topics for elective classes change from semester to semester. The focus might be on illustration, three-dimensional models, sculpture, pottery, fabric, or a particular genre of painting. More extensive electives can include planning a science fair (although the emphasis is on working together as a team of teams to insure that all students are appreciated for their contributions) or connecting community service work with social studies. Simpler electives might be the study of geography based on reading the daily newspaper, or one of our all-time favorites, chocolate chip math, where you get to eat the correct answers.

The other important avenue for extensive projects takes place during what is called group time. This is when one's own age group meets regularly. How often is not the same from year to year, because of pressures to cover specific topics more traditionally. Meetings might take place only once a week, or there might be four meetings. As well, the overall goals vary from teacher to teacher. However, the general design, toward which most of the teachers aim, is to embed the full range of the curriculum in a comprehensive project that is planned by the teacher and the students together over the period of a semester. The goal is to integrate many subjects into accomplishing the project. The role of the teachers, though an occasional lecture is not ruled out, is far removed from basic traditional methods of teaching. The success of the project depends on how well student-directed learning is facilitated. Whether students are working individually or in small groups, it is a major goal of the Project Learn community that children learn to work independently of their teachers. Of equal significance, it is inherent in group work that children will develop affective skills related to listening, regarding, discussing, adjusting, and asserting their needs in cooperation with others. Ideally, the project is experienced by each child as his or her own as well as each of the group mates. It is rewarding that this is usually the case.

One time, a very popular group project was the study of chocolate chip cookies. It involved learning the history of the cookie, the farming, the manufacturing, and the distribution of the ingredients—from the source to baking to eating. It involved history, geography, sociology, math, and science. The children worked in small groups to bake cookies with commercially prepared ingredients and then with ones that they had made from scratch. They learned that the wheat they ground themselves makes much coarser cookies and their chocolate chips were strange to say the least. But in unraveling such a common part of their daily lives, they were able to develop really integrated knowledge and sensibility for a small but important part of their lives. Besides, they got some firsthand experience about capitalism when they offered the cookies for sale to other children in the school.

For another group, *Going Places*, a guide to children's activities in Philadelphia, was written and published as a result of extensive field research into resources for having fun in the city with a parent or on your own. In the arts, a sculpture installation was modeled after the work of Judy Chicago with a ceramic place setting created by each student. Each child made a painting of a woman in history or one who was personally important to the student. It was installed at a local gallery filled with tables displaying the place settings and the walls covered with paintings of significant women in the history of the children. An extra-large annual yard sale, the work of the junior high for many years, became a significant fundraiser for the school—involving the collection, pricing, organizing, setting up, entertainment, refreshments, selling, taking down, and making enough money to tap the parent-run fundraising committee's jealousy. Simpler excitement and fun for children came from asking a world traveler to carry a teddy bear with a knapsack full of postcards. Arriving at the destination, one of the postcards was sent back to Project Learn with news of the bear's travels, and then the bear was handed off to another traveler. The postcards became a lesson in geography and history.

Teachers must take care to agree to projects that are in the realm of their interests and basic skills; and as well, they must be consistent with the learning goals that are held for their students. Being an expert isn't necessary. Indeed, knowing too much about a project can handicap the excitement attached to a teacher's learning. The curricular task is to design projects with students that challenge them to further develop a range of skills including a combination of reading, writing, math, the arts, science, social studies, and history. Not all projects foster every one of these, but all of them include some of them. Much of this work depends upon responsible movement around the classroom, the building, and in the community. The emphasis is on their independent learning, occasionally alone for a time, but mostly in small groups. Teachers too have to think about making an honest contribution to the projects. Altogether, there is an opportunity to find out that age is not the only factor that makes for smart. And, during group time while working with peers, students have many opportunities to develop age-appropriate social skills along with their intellectual learning.

P. L. PAPER

Authentic choice is the key to matching manageable challenges with a high potential for successful accomplishments. From an educational standpoint, this matching is what it means to meet students' needs. The support of this authenticity requires teachers to contend with the problem of balancing respect for a student's wishes with intuitions about the feasibility of success. A good example is the work involved in producing the school newspaper. This is one of the electives that gets closest to meeting the plethora of needs with which children come to school—much because the work is so varied. But, mostly because of the process of teaching and learning that has evolved. During a period when Donna and Barbara Glass (now Sweeny) were team teaching this elective, Rich Quinn, a parent, commented at the town meeting that the school newspaper wasn't really students' work. It was too good, he said. He was sure that the quality resulted from the teachers' contributions to each article. His comments were met with a hard put challenge: show up for a few classes to observe firsthand and then judge for himself.

Rich was correct, the teachers' work makes a critical difference, but not in the way he imagined. Just witnessing a team of two teachers and fifteen students as young as eight for a few days was enough to understand how a teacher can bring together a democratic teaching process with the production of a high-quality newspaper. At the very start, the class examines and discusses newspapers with the help of a parent who was a professor of journalism. Following this, as always, the next issue is initiated with a brainstorming session. The big question is what do we think is newsworthy right now? The students are instructed to think along the lines of school news connected with class work, extracurricular activities, the running of the school, members of the Project Learn community (current students, alumni, teachers, parents, family life, and extended families) and the local community. Each child is expected to write a news item and a feature—events that have taken place and a story about someone, some place, or a book review. If the teachers feel there isn't enough material, children are sent off in teams to talk with other teachers and the secretary in search of more stories.

Once all the choices are listed on newsprint and posted, the children bid for the stories they want to write. If there is more than one person, a simple lottery takes place—nothing more complicated than pick a number from one to twenty. At this point, the teachers have been known to do a little fudging, but we're not going to talk about it. The aim is to make sure that students get their first choice more than once a semester. A large number of listed possibilities have helped the process work out. With their choices in hand, the students are then asked to write at least ten questions for each of the two articles and to include who they think should be interviewed. They are asked to address at least six kinds of questions: who, what, where, when, why, and how. In a detailed discussion with the class as a whole, the questions for each student are critiqued. They are improved, and likely as not, a few more questions are added. Then, the discussion returns to who should be interviewed for each article. Together, the teachers and the students evaluate where each writer might get the best help. Outside of class, they find the people or call from school or home and make appointments.

After each interview, and maybe tracking down other information, students report back with a copy of their first draft. These are read aloud and discussed. The class then suggests other questions that might be asked and other kinds of information that would make the story more interesting and complete. A second draft follows, and this time it is critiqued by one of the teachers. All spelling is corrected. The teachers struggle with how much the child's work may be edited for grammar and sentence structure, but care is taken to make sure that students' work is their own. Students write their final draft themselves. The result is that some of the articles are more mature than others, but all of it is honestly authored by the students. What the children don't do is sell space to advertisers from the community, build a list of outside subscribers, prepare photos for the copy that goes to the printer, layout, or arrange for the printing. But, they do the work of delivering the paper to the students and teachers in school and preparing the mailing to the other subscribers. Numerous times the *P. L. Paper* has won scholastic awards for excellence, and for three years in a row, it merited the highest award given for schools in its class, nationally. The children who work on the paper feel pride in their writing and have good reason to be proud of themselves. When it arrives back from the printer, every child first turns to his or her articles. It's a good moment.

EVALUATION

On the Opinions page, an occasional -section appearing in the *P. L. Paper*, this is what Jonathan Cox (1984) had to say just before his graduation:

> Since coming to Project Learn, I have become more open to other people and how we can help each other. I have learned a lot from my studies, teachers, and friends. It was hard to accept responsibility for myself and it was a lesson I learned at P. L. The teachers made me accept what I had to do for no one would do it for me. Working with my friends to make something work was a lesson I will have for life. The important thing was friendship between teachers and students and each other.

The care and concern for each other was more than during the school day. I feel I can always come back to P. L. to friends.

With a bit of reframing, one can notice that this is Jonathan's big picture of what he learned at Project Learn. When thinking about evaluating children's schoolwork, it would be normal not to count this thoughtful reflection as more than an opinion, which is what it is. Even at Project Learn, it might not be taken more seriously by some. Reviewing old issues of the *P. L. Paper* for the writing of this chapter, and stumbling on Jonathan's "opinion," we realized that this is where the evaluation process begins and ends—for and with the self. What did I learn in school, he asks of himself? And, this is his answer. He points out that he succeeded academically in the context of learning how to take responsibility, working together with other students, and valuing friendships with peers and mentors. This he says was a life lesson. And although his writing might have been more polished, the lesson learned is impressive.

But "begins and ends" does not exclude a complex and valuable middle ground that is the official story of the evaluation process at Project Learn. Tests of all sorts are given during the course of a semester, and creative work is critiqued. However, the results do not become part of a cumulative grade; their purpose is to evaluate how well children understand their lessons so far. They provide feedback to both the students and the teachers. The students have to ask whether they are studying hard enough; the teachers have to wonder whether their teaching is sufficiently helpful, in general and with regard to specific students. Both have to ask what they would need of themselves and others to do a better job. Some subjects lend themselves to objective questions like, how well have the multiplication tables been learned or do the students remember the facts covered in a science or history lesson? Reading comprehension is evaluated by questioning children about what they have read. Work in some subjects creates a paper trail of written work or artistic creation; here, though clearly subjective, the quality can be judged by a teacher's standards. Writing published in the *P. L. Paper* is open for all to see and judge. And altogether, this material, the artifacts of learning, is used as the basis of regular discussions. Weekly, if not daily, students and teachers are confronted with the failures and successes that demonstrate how well their goals are being achieved.

Goals are highlighted. Teachers and parents, together with the student, attend conferences twice or more times a year and goals on everyone's part are articulated and shared, compared, and evaluated. The teachers, as would they anywhere, can't get them out of their minds. Some are written, some just spoken but clear, and then some are muddy, unconscious workings of the mind. Parents have them, although they are not usually written, and they run a similar gamut. And even if during the course of a semester, students don't have them in mind at all, they usually can voice them with encouragement. With teachers' notes and logs in hand and in the presence of the student's artifacts, everyone has a say about what has been accomplished, what needs special attention in the upcoming semester, and how well goals have been achieved. Students, too, are expected to voice their opinions with regard to their achievements, lack of progress, and what needs to be done. And, teachers make a great effort to insure that students hear, in addition to they what need to do, appreciation for their accomplishments and their strengths.

What happens next is what doesn't happen. Nothing in the process turns an evaluation of the student's learning into grades. Not even pass or fail. The concepts of grades, passing, and failing are outside the pale of the Project Learn's philosophy of education. The focus on goals is to help insure that the final judge of learning is each individual student. Substantial efforts are made to discourage children from basing judgments about their learning on comparisons with the learning of other students. The counter-argument is about how this isn't the way it happens in the real world—the fact of competition is the bottom-line lesson. The parents, teachers, and children at Project Learn have been satisfied with their experience that achieving personal goals is an effective path to immediate success. They bank on its value for the future.

It is understood that students' personal goals will not necessarily reflect those of the parents, the teachers, the community, and the larger contexts. But, there is plenty of room for influencing what and how goals are set, particularly when students are expected to think and respected for thinking on their own. In practical terms, the constant critiquing of children's work, giving honest feedback and support, makes grading unnecessary. The advantage is that students don't have an official basis for comparing themselves with others, which in the real world is not productive. Students aren't given the opportunity to get stuck in the idea of being a poor student or a good one. Flexibility is engendered for approaching new lessons with the focus on immediate successes, even small ones, rather than worrying about improvement or maintenance of a record, bad or good. Both have disadvantages. A star student has a reputation to uphold; a slow student is always fighting for self-esteem. Marking students saps the energy for learning, weighing it down with psychological baggage—even when it's good news. Outside of school, with a stake in one's future, the practical skills needed are the ability to set realistic goals, accept feedback, and use the feedback as a tool for improving performance. Learning to do this without being defensive is a tough, valuable life lesson. This is a large part of what Jonathan learned.

The problem of passing or failing doesn't come up because, not only are children not graded, they are not precisely grouped in grades either. At the end of the year, teachers discuss each student's skills, both academic and social. They reflect on the wishes of the child. From this, compatible groups are formed for the next year, roughly comparable in size, that include overlapping ages. Normal cultural pressures push the kids to figure out what grade they are in, at the least to tell friends who don't go to Project Learn. Mainly though, it is not a big issue in the daily life of the school. The students mix freely when they are in elective classes, and the school is small (only 100 students today) so that every child knows all of the other children. There is little room for feeling that one is in the wrong class. So, when a child is assigned to the same teacher as the year before, it is highly unlikely to be an embarrassing event. Students find themselves in groups that are comfortable and reasonably challenging learning environments. Teachers, too, typically don't repeat their lessons from year to year, taking time to refresh their methods and offer variations of the curriculum.

There are times when parents and teachers will push for changes in the curriculum that offset some of the humanistic aspects of the program. Some are not problematic. Students do need experience taking standardized tests. The compromise was to administer them to anyone who wants the experience. The students get a chance to talk about how to improve their performance, but the tests are not totaled. No opportunity is created for comparing the results of the tests locally or otherwise. When a student graduates and applies to a high school that requires a standardized entrance examination, this practice is especially useful. Other times, a high school will require a record of letter grades—in addition to the written evaluations that are a normal part of a student's records. A teacher will translate the record into grades in discussion with the student. If the high school needs more information, it is assumed that the admission's officer will turn to the descriptive record. By the time students graduate from Project Learn, the staff is confident that a decision made with their parents of where to apply is likely to be in line with a realistic appraisal of their abilities. Usually, students apply to special magnet schools that touch interests they have developed in their elementary and junior high education. If anything, graduating students have more informed abilities to make choices about their education than is typical.

Problematic are pressures to alter the curriculum in the direction of more traditional school programs. The early hope was that young children wouldn't be taught to read and do math until they expressed interest. The idea fits with progressive theories and research about the need for readiness. The idea was too foreign for even the progressive parents who committed themselves to this adventure in humanistic education. A higher order humanistic tenet is that the concerns of people come before the ideas about education. To this day, the children are taught these skills not radically different than they would be in any other school—though not with the same pressures occurring most elsewhere, when they are of kindergarten age. There is some leeway, but nowhere near what had been the hope. In later years, there have been other changes to respond to parents' or teachers' worries about not enough science, computer literacy, foreign language, music, or physical education. There is nothing intrinsically wrong with adding these subjects, but the problem it creates is an overloaded curriculum that reduces opportunities for group time. It's not as if teachers in most cases don't want both, but the reality of less time stands unless there is a willingness to give something up.

What has been encouraging over the years is that the Project Learn curriculum has remained flexible. Changes go back and forth, not without a struggle in staff meetings and in town meetings, but they are part of the school's culture. Why? Parents and teachers, old ones and new ones, understand that the character of the school depends on two of its basic humanistic tenets. One, critical aspects of the infrastructure have been supported by a firm belief in consensus—by the ever-changing faculty and parent body. Consensus gets an occasional pounding, but it's still staunchly standing in place. Two, the idea that a student's learning should not be compared with others at least on the basis of grades has in fact never been challenged. Furthermore, what carries this humanistic program along in large part is the community belief that everyone is responsible when children aren't learning: parents, teachers, and children. Keeping a structure that respectfully honors the contributions of everyone maintains the life energy that sustains the school. A belief in the value of honoring each individual's needs first is required—somehow working out compromises that don't compromise integrity.

The real world does pass and fail. However, nature's strategy for young humans born incapable of caring for themselves, from an evolutionary standpoint, is to require protection and nurturance for children in a safe environment for many years. The adults at Project Learn are cognizant of the many opportunities to learn difficult lessons about failure that abound. Many have occurred already, and many more are around the bend, soon enough. The philosophy holds to making sure, as is humanly possible, that the failures that occur are not so great as to undermine the development of a sense of agency. The aim is to insure a strong history of successful accomplishments, overall, and particularly some that bear on shaping one's own education. Some may ask whether Project Learn students succeeded in life worse, the same, or better than children who were educated elsewhere? Given the philosophy, there is no possibility that their education in this school will be measured and compared by traditional grades. What we know is that in the years since Jonathan Cox graduated, he hasn't come back to say he didn't get the education he needed and deserved as a young child. Now, after nearly forty years, those who have come back only say it was a very special school. Bravo for the parents, the teachers, and the students.

2

Establishing Boundaries

Establishing boundaries in the classroom is one key to becoming the kind of teacher one wants to be. For too many teachers, though, this is nothing more than announcing a set of rules that defines good behavior. Inexperienced teachers worry, with just cause, about being overwhelmed by behavior problems that are often profound. Based on these early fears, many teachers with years of experience continue to imagine that they can control students with rules. Yet, it is not abnormal to fail at holding them hard and fast. Too often, teachers make rules that they constantly feel unable to carry out. Unfortunately, behavior problems have become an accepted part of classroom experience. No teacher will be fired simply because they occur. All that is expected is a reasonable level of control.

To make matters worse, blame exacerbates the infraction of rules. Even when we know who is at fault it isn't easy, but if just one student feels unjustly accused, true or untrue, the situation is likely to get difficult. We don't need to say what happens when many students feel they are being treated unjustly. The situation escalates when a child or a class really gets out of control. Teachers, parents, or both, now qualify as targets to be blamed. Once the battle gets going, any stakeholder is likely to be held responsible. The problem may have its beginning in poor school leadership, inadequate resources provided by the community or the state, or misguided standards set by the federal government. There is tremendous pressure to name who is causing the trouble. Everyone including the students wants a better deal. And, at every level, it is fair (a complicated word itself) to ask who (singular or plural) is irresponsible.

It is assumed that there needs to be a constant awareness of the rules, and this is accompanied by a pervasive threat of punishment, which is a common theme in too many school cultures. This culture runs contrary to the notion of school as a supportive environment for taking risks. Some rules must exist and punishment is sometimes in order. The problem, however, is the dominant ambience of distrust that is created. Added to the distrust is how teachers inconsistently follow through with consequences set for breaking the rules. Hereby, regular reminders of the struggle between teachers and students are repeated. What is too often missing is movement in the direction of realizing the higher personal ideals about teaching and learning. Teachers are expected to teach their students effectively even though being the teacher one wants to be is thwarted.

There is too much emphasis on rules and not enough about a process that invites cooperation—what we call establishing boundaries. Paradoxically, why are there some teachers who are able to smile before Christmas? For us, light begins to shine on the question when we remember that there are teachers, everywhere, who seem to have a bit of magic in their touch. Without a strong emphasis on rules or threats, with a true lightness in speaking, all it usually takes for them is, "please stop what you are doing and get to work." Indeed, most teachers get to experience this at least once in a while. We miss the relevance of the magic when we say, "this is a good student" or "this is a great class." When conflicts arise, insight is gained by analyzing the source of the struggle, not declaring this is a bad class. No teacher has this magic all of the time. Ease in the classroom is not the result of a class run with an iron hand. It's more like intelligent classroom management. The value of this understanding is to recognize that the teacher who has ease is always in the process of building his or her relationship with the students, and helping them to do the same with each other.

While rules send the unreliable message that the relationship with the teacher can be clearly understood by eliminating a set of undesirable behaviors, setting boundaries involves the work of building a relationship. We look at the establishment of boundaries as the foundational element of a classroom that is designed to meet the needs of all the students. There is then a better chance of providing a satisfying and pleasurable environment for the teacher and the students. There is room in the process to come to agreements whereby students are encouraged to buy into established boundaries. The teacher remains responsible for the outer limits—the safety and well-being of the students and the creation of the learning environment. The teacher is still responsible for creating an attractive set of lessons and requiring reasonable means of evaluation. The simplest element that draws students in is to offer choices where the integrity of the program will not be compromised and may even be enhanced. The more difficult element is to encourage feedback about the social and intellectual structure of the classroom and to be open to making changes, sometimes for particular student needs and sometimes for the class as a whole. All the while, attention has to be paid to making sure that the structure as a whole satisfies the teacher's needs.

That children will be treated differently is one of the more contentious ideas we propose. Fairness is not about treating children equally; it is a matter of meeting their needs without infringing on others. The day that Donna had to deal with Penny coming to Project Learn with a switchblade is a dramatic example.

Penny rode a long way on the Germantown Avenue trolley to come to school, all the way from north Philadelphia. It was a Monday in September before classes began when the knife appeared, and one of the children came lickety-split to get Donna, who was in the office. "It may be hard to imagine how fast I moved to the second floor to find her." They went back to the office and the conversation went something like this:

> DONNA: Penny, you may not bring a knife to school.
> PENNY: There is no way I'm coming on the trolley without my knife.
> D: But, Penny, it is not possible for you to have a knife in school.
> P: Well, I won't come without it. I wouldn't be safe.
> D: Do you feel safe at school?
> P: Sort of, but you never know when someone might mess with you.

The conversation continued for a while, and it became clear that Penny was really frightened to come to school unprotected. She had no real experience feeling safe even in school. It was obvious to Donna that this knife was so important to this eleven-year-old child that if she forbade her, she would sneak it in somehow. Donna made a deal with her. She told her that upon arrival at school she would give the knife to her until she left for home and promised that if anyone messed with her, regular school would be stopped so that everyone could talk about it. Penny wasn't fully satisfied that Donna could keep her safe, but she agreed. Her mother was called, and she was told about their plan. For a week or so, Penny brought the knife every morning, and it was returned to her at the end of the day. Donna is unsure of what happened then, but at the end of the year, she found the knife at the back of her desk drawer. She asked Penny what she wanted to do with the knife. Penny told her that she could toss it out.

It's true that the story has a rosy end; not all do. Still, it teaches us how boundaries have to be both firm yet with some give to them. The boundary set that there could be no weapons in school worked. Penny felt safe enough, and Donna felt not too uncomfortable having a knife in the desk drawer. They negotiated what worked for both of them. No rule in the world would have thwarted Penny from her need for safety, and the school would have lost her before they got rid of the knife. Does this example fit today for other schools, or even Project Learn, in a time far removed from the 1970s? Unknown, but the lesson of adjusting boundaries still stands. There are other moments when a student steps so far outside the boundaries that the teacher takes charge by interrupting the normal work of the classroom, or the entire school. When a teacher feels that a conflict cannot be taken in stride, it is time to stop. Often, it becomes a community problem, not a matter of blaming students. It may seem impractical in the face of a habitually difficult classroom; there would be no time at all left for learning. We ignore the truth, though, by not admitting that this is already the case. Until there is a sense of a functioning social order, a school community or a teacher might as well spend the time it takes to build one.

It takes time and strategic leadership on the part of the teacher to establish and maintain effective boundaries. Content-driven classrooms are hard pressed to take the time needed to honestly make the effort to get and keep all of the students on board. Instead of defining a truce, however, it's worth taking the risk of having boundaries in which learning takes place in a contactful and meaningful way for all students. And, whenever the process is not conducive to learning, teachers will discover that the content can be effectively interrupted without a greater loss of learning than happens in any class. Of course, the teacher uses his or her normal authority to ask students to stop making a commotion and pay attention. But when this authority breaks down, it makes no sense to continue addressing the content—when in fact there can be very little learning happening. It is not only more humanistic to focus on the process when too much is happening, it is practical and efficient.

For teachers and students, there is also a subtle negotiation of each other's power. Students have their own source of threat, not to be ignored. Again, in practical terms, no matter how disinterested a teacher is in humanistic teaching, to dismiss the power of students in the balance is courting trouble. At worst, students take pleasure in making a teacher's life miserable. The smart teacher avoids engagement on this level. The greatest success of the teacher depends upon the students' applying themselves with a fullness of spirit to achieve. This is what counts most as a teacher's achievement. Only the students can do this.

More optimistically, though all relationships of any value are murky waters, time and attention to differences and common interests clarify them. The traditional assumption about rules so inherent in teaching ironically sets up the conditions for the struggle—without a hint of resolution. In contrast, teachers who manage their classrooms with ease are able to maintain an attitude that normal daily problems are meant to be taken in stride. For them, classroom experience is not essentially a matter of rules. What happens is based on the time taken to build mutually supportive relationships with the students and among them; the emphasis is on partnerships that serve to resolve the conflicts that occur. Teaching in this way replaces most of the rules with the belief that children as well as the adults are partners in designing, planning, and carrying out their education. They are not equal partners but still partners.

Boundaries in the making are aimed at providing the teacher and the students with an ongoing process that makes it possible to come to agreement. The time it takes means not covering as much of the material on any given day. But covering material, as a strategy, like abiding by the rules, is shortsighted. While rules tend to separate teachers from the concerns of the students, relationships heighten understanding of each other. It behooves teachers to go beyond the fears that children will go outside the boundaries, fearing that a point will be reached where they cannot be brought back within acceptable limits. What is required is believing in the students' underlying commitment to their own learning and sufficient sense of responsibility. These qualities are needed for competent learning, and as well, it is the teacher's belief in students that makes a great deal of difference whether commitment and responsibility will come to the surface. A teacher who takes this position is in a better place to know more about who their students really are. There can be an understanding confidence in children as individuals that is cognizant of their potential, in the eyes of both the teacher and the students.

But be warned: these ideas are not easy solutions. There are no silver bullets. Some situations are beyond hope. There is nothing to negotiate without a vital educational program to offer. If students have only negativity to offer, change may not be possible. And, of utmost significance are the teacher's strengths. Common sense about what "I" the teacher might be able to do successfully is the real starting point. These ideas only make sense to the degree that a teacher organizes them into personal, living educational theory (Whitehead, 1993). This is a theory where "I" takes responsibility, just as we expect students to do. Furthermore, this text itself must be translated and embodied in the realities of a teacher's personal practice.

TWO-SIDED REPORT CARDS

More will be accomplished if students are committed to the established boundaries. In moments of planning or stress, the teacher can ask the class: What do we as a group do when one of us goes outside the boundaries we have set? What do we expect from one another? How do we help a person who was part of the process come back to the goals of the group? There are valid peer pressures, and there are valid limits that a teacher must assert. Because they are not part of an essentially rule-based community, students can push back. Students need to be part of a community, but if teachers lack the faith in their ability to waken that need in their students, teaching will be quite an empty task. To take time and risks is what education is supposed to be. No coach would expect less from the players; classroom teachers do best to ask of their students to be part of an effective team. Better than a sports team, everyone stands to win. In a successful classroom there is a mix of complexity and simplicity. The general tension is symbolized in the traditional two-sided report card used in elementary schools. On one page, the grade for each subject studied appears. On the facing page, ratings are given for deportment (as it was called when we were in school), conduct, or behavior. The division is taken for granted. The representation of educational goals and classroom behavior is literally not on the same page. Instead of worrying where one compensates for the other, even if this split marking system is required, the teacher can conceptualize them as two sides of the same mind. Establishing boundaries then involves discussion and planning with children in an effort to find out how a mutually acceptable set of goals can be achieved. To accomplish them obviously involves behaviors, not rules. The process is about their education, not separate from classroom behavior.

STAFF DEVELOPMENT

Learning to be a humanistic teacher requires new ways of thinking. This was painfully apparent in the early days of Project Learn. Too often, traditional patterns of teaching arose out of either past teaching experience or what was learned from years of being a student experiencing teaching. Failing ideals in the face of classroom conflicts all too quickly brought out these old patterns instead of an integrated response that interconnected children's behavior, the educational program, and the needs of the students and the teachers. In retrospect, we can see how teachers were behaving defensively. Should someone in class get way out of line, the first thought was to think there was something wrong with the child, and the "correct" answer was that he or she just needed more attention. In the progressive spirit of the times, teachers quite simply gave the culprit an overabundance of adult time and attention. Unnoticed was how much this accepted solution didn't help to ameliorate the situation. Neither punishment nor reward was the answer. In those moments, Project Learn on the surface looked like other schools when teachers were frustrated with their students' behavior.

It was actually a young child who boldly provided an insight much like it happened in the story of the emperor with no clothes. One morning, Tim, who in general was quite a remarkable nine-year old, started acting awful. He started by yelling. He knocked down a model built by a small group of his classmates. He then hit a few children. He was truly awful—in no way like the child he had been before. Donna, his teacher, took him aside and asked, "Tim, what is going on?" The dialogue went something like this: "Well, Donna, I've been watching, and I noticed that when John acted this way, he got to do a lot of fun things that the rest of us didn't get to do. So, I figured if I acted like John, I'd get more attention and have fun too." Tim made it obvious that the teachers needed to find more creative ways to teach, beginning with being smarter.

Getting on Tim's wavelength was easy enough. It was also easy enough to see that an overabundance of attention as a set response wasn't any better than administering routine punishments for breaking a set of rules. Donna realized too that Tim wasn't the real problem; she knew it was John. Letting his behavior slide conveyed a message that the social organization of the class was not functioning up to par. And, the idea of stopping the normal flow of a class lesson and raising questions about the process, as she did with Tim, weren't foreign to her. She already knew this was necessary at times. Yet, something was getting in the way.

Consciously or not, Donna was in a bind because experience had taught her that teaching of any kind is undermined if every two minutes the focus on learning is interrupted by the students—or the teacher. This is a practical consideration in every classroom, no matter what philosophy of education is being used as a guide. This common sense had blocked her from stopping the normal classroom process earlier. But more critically, she vividly remembers that the intelligence, intuitions, and confidence so often available to her were sometimes being drawn into conflict with habits formed from years of seeing teaching done differently. More so, this was happening to all of the teachers at Project Learn. Not when all was going well, but when there were problems. Across the board, there was difficulty and confusion about acting outside the mold of traditional teaching.

Quite consciously, common sense also pointed toward the need for staff development. Though such educational programs are often disappointing, then as now, the hope was that the teachers at Project Learn could learn to inhibit traditional behaviors in favor of ones that supported their humanistic ideals. Nothing less seemed reasonable, especially as a model for the children who themselves were expected to let go of their stereotypes of school. Youngsters playing school routinely put the kids in rows while the "teacher" stands in front of them, pointing, asking questions, giving answers, and pontificating rules—with threats of punishment should the rules be broken. However, in-service programs in the 1970s, though innovative, weren't sufficiently different from this traditional mold.

Dennis Sparks and Susan Loucks-Horsley (1990), discussing the earlier programs, outlined their aims as essentially a variety of models for improving teaching methods and classroom management. Established as an avenue for teacher self-development—with names, in addition to staff development, such as in-service training, teacher development, and professional development—they contributed to the creation of needed innovative teaching techniques and new approaches to behavior problems. Improving these skills was necessary but not sufficient. None aimed at the development of teacher-student relationships—needed skills for the interactive dialogue in which the teachers at Project Learn were attempting to engage.

The new ways of thinking required both intellectual and emotional learning that paralleled the development of the self that takes place in psychotherapy. But then again, such methods are inappropriate for staff development unless they can be quite distinct from psychotherapy. There is a fine line between exploring the personal space of daily life and the emotionally laden experiences of professional work. At the time, William Glasser (1969) was promoting workshops for teachers in classes with their students that demonstrated how this separation is possible. Using his skills as a psychiatrist, he led practical classroom meetings that incorporated children's feelings to show directly how improvements in the social environment could lead to increased harmony and learning. Meeting with teachers outside of their classes, he trained them how to provide this kind of leadership themselves. Glasser's success raised confidence that teachers could be expected to explore the emotional space of children without crossing over the line into psychotherapy. Good news, but still not sufficient. Because the Project Learn staff was more concerned with navigating the establishment of permissive boundaries rather than about an emphasis on following a set of restrictive rules, the problem was as much about the teacher's behavior as it was about the students.

Brad Blanton, a colleague from our days at Miami University, introduced us to Gestalt therapy. Its central focus was on the context of experience, which seemed to be particularly amenable to a model of staff development that would stay within the realm of educational concerns. Though this therapeutic approach had been introduced twenty years prior by Frederick Perls, Ralph Hefferline, and Paul Goodman (1951), there were now widespread discussions breaking into the mainstream of psychology. Brad was excited about how this approach emphasized taking personal responsibility for guiding one's actions and had taken advantage of an opportunity to train with Perls. He supported our hunch that the techniques of Gestalt therapy could be applied to classroom teaching and learning. At Brad's invitation, Donna enrolled in an experiential workshop he was leading and returned enthused.

Paralleling the evolution of education, the traditional canon of psychology was finally giving way to change. The humanism that Freud brought to psychological thought had become too dogmatic for the modern world, ruling out other possibilities for thinking about mental health. The favorite contender was Skinnerian reinforcement theory. The former devalued conscious thinking; the latter ignored how the human mind thinks at all. Dissatisfied with these two polar approaches to emotional learning, psychologists including Perls and his colleagues were exploring alternatives.

Ironically, it was the discussions of learning theory by Hartmann, Kaffka, Kohler, and others in Germany in the 1920s and 1930s, not related to emotions at all, that set the stage for understanding the role of context in both intellectual and emotional learning. Classical Gestalt theory (Hilgard, 1948) challenged the behavioristic concept that learning was mainly associations strengthened by reinforcement. Context meant seeing both figure and ground—like the drawing of the old lady/young lady reproduced in psychology textbooks for decades. What is figural in our minds is dependent upon what is in present awareness. When we ask children to focus on some aspect of learning, we are really asking that they make the lesson figural. Thinking about what is perceived and thinking itself, argued the early Gestalt psychologists, are the major mechanics of learning. From these arguments, learning theory has radically been expanding ever since.

This cognitive psychology attracted Perls and his colleagues, both the strength of its challenge to psychological theory and the concept of figure and ground. They struggled with the choice between Freudian psychology and behaviorism, both of which were unacceptable to them. Perls saw the concept of figure and ground as the foundation of Gestalt therapy. The expanded relevance to emotional learning proved to be even more fundamental than when the sole focus was on intellectual experience. Psychotherapy in his mind required attention to the interaction of the two. George Brown (1971), whose significant influences included Maslow and Rogers as well as Perls, saw the interweaving of intellectual and emotional experiences equally critical for the purpose of humanistic education.

Brown coined the term *confluent learning* to represent, "the integration or flowing together of the affective and cognitive elements in individual and group learning" (Brown, p. 3). The needs of students and teachers are never limited solely to the intellectual goals that are held. Emotional concerns play a major role in enabling cognitive learning to flourish and succeed, and beyond this immediate context, there is emotional learning itself that is appropriate in connection with motivation, learning to work together, and acquiring skills for future learning. The roots and the promise of Gestalt theory were in place; now was the time to apply the theory to practice. The staff development program was designed using this theoretical framework.

TRAINING FOR EASE

In consultation with the Project Learn staff, Donna enrolled in a program for training Gestalt therapists—with the express purpose of applying her learning to staff development. The staff supported her absence from school several weeks throughout the year. During the same year, the staff structured two meetings every week, one for administrative and educational planning and the other for the work of becoming humanistic teachers. One school day was shortened to allow for one meeting; parents were asked to cover classes for the other. Given the enthusiasm of those early days and interest in the project, enough people found the time to pitch in. The success enjoyed established the attitude about teachers' responsibilities that still functions in its own way to this day.

Staff resistance to the Gestalt meetings, however, was also en-countered. At various times different teachers felt exposed and de-fensive; the psychological exposure, though boundaried, was chal-lenging for all of us. Added to the stress were disagreements about priorities that the teachers faced in planning a high-quality educa-tional program. Yet, we persevered and for five years exciting new horizons were forged with relative ease. We gained a culture of teachers exploring their responsibility to create an effective hu-manistic learning environment for every child in the school. There has been a gradual decrease in the amount of time for doing this intense kind of self-study, but the legacy of the founding teachers still influences the culture of today's staff.

Some of the staff development meetings involved opportunities to try out these concepts through role-playing. The work, which was far more intense, offered staff members the opportunity to dis-cuss specific problems they were facing with an individual child, a small group, or even the class as a whole. The goal of this work was to discover how the child or the group might be better served. This was accomplished by helping the teacher develop an under-standing of what in the environment was causing the problem. Sometimes, after many attempts to change the classroom environ-ment, it was necessary to think about whether the structure of Project Learn worked for a child. However, the starting point as-sumed that it was the teacher's responsibility to make changes to accommodate the student's needs.

The sessions began with the teacher describing the problem. The whole staff discussed what was happening and how the other teachers experienced the child or group. Everyone was encouraged to express his or her feelings about the situation. Teachers often discovered their fear of loss of control or their own sense of shame when they were students. When we identified our feelings, we were better able to act differently when those feelings were again trig-gered in the classroom. The staff would brainstorm ideas for changes that the teacher could make in the classroom environ-ment or in the teacher's behavior. The following week we would check in to see if our creative ideas did in fact have a positive ef-fect and if not we would start again. There was a real sense of col-legiality and cooperation among the staff and very little sense of criticism or blame about having a problem. We felt safe in reveal-ing what in other places may have been viewed as our failures. At these meetings, they were viewed as works in progress.

We don't recall any specific incidents or students that we worked on in those early years, but we do remember the staff member who could not tolerate the idea that she had to change.

She made it very clear that it was either the school climate or the child who was at fault for any problem she had. No matter how hard we all worked to suggest gently that she might try to work in a different way or even to think about what it was about the child that bothered her so much, she refused. She knew that what she was doing was working well for most of the children so it must be that the problem child was really at fault. It mattered not at all that every other teacher was doing really well most of the time, but that we knew it was our responsibility to serve all the children, even the ones who did not respond to our "great" lessons. This teacher did not stay at Project Learn very long; she returned to what she called a regular school.

The Gestalt exercises were more fun for the staff. They were designed to explore and challenge the ideas and underlying beliefs we have about teaching and being teachers. Often the exercises put two beliefs at odds to discover the place between them that is most lively and engaging for the teacher. We had to come to terms with what was ideal and what was possible. Some exercises asked us to uncover our assumptions about our students and ourselves. We were often shocked by what we had assumed about another person. Usually the work was done in pairs and sometimes as a whole group. We laughed a lot during this part of the meetings when our own conflicting ideas were revealed, and it was not so hard to learn from the exercise.

A big underlying belief we hold as teachers involves how we *should* be as teachers and how students *should* be. When we were asked to say, "Yes, they should," or "No, they shouldn't," to statements such as, "Teachers should always grade and return students' work by the next day." Or, "Students should always hand in their homework the day after it was assigned." Or, "Students should always listen to the teacher." Or, "Teachers should always listen to the students." Our own internal conflicts were exposed. As much as we laughed at the absurdity of the "always" statements, they forced us to look at the places in-between. How does each person feel heard and respected without limiting the other? When is it appropriate to limit the other? How do we balance the needs of the teacher and the students? And very importantly, which of the *shoulds* interfere with being a humanistic teacher? Sometimes we pondered where we got these shoulds. "Students should sit quietly in the classroom, preferably in straight rows in alphabetical order!" Hmmm?

Looking at our expectations of children and our preconceived notions about them helped us to realize that much of what we placed on them is what we expected of ourselves or what was expected of us as students. Because Donna's mother expected her to take at least two years of Latin does not mean that she should expect it of her students. When we realized the origin of our assumptions, we were able to make different choices for students and ourselves.

As part of the work, we had opportunities among the staff to express resentments and appreciations, which cleared the air for us to work closely together. We learned about listening in exercises where we had to repeat what we had seen and heard in an enactment of a classroom scene. And, we learned about how daily we resist using the human resources available to us, because we believe we are supposed to do it all on our own. The exercises that involved asking for help were the most difficult. Occasionally, we would say to a teacher, "You are required to ask for help from one of us everyday this week." That task was difficult for some, but it led to a deeper connection among the staff members.

Although now there are no regular, separate meetings to work on the Gestalt exercises, it is remarkable to be able to report that there are teachers at Project Learn who continue the tradition of self-study. Nancy Bailey, though retired, teaches every morning, and Lisa Pack, our sister-in-law who was a volunteer for a year at age seventeen and later returned as a mother and a teacher, take lunch time for self-study. They review problems and look at how they have not met the needs of specific children. Both value the opportunity to explore their teaching and how they serve the children. Their energy spills over to other staff members who join them occasionally with their problems.

It is true that only a small portion of today's regular staff meetings deals with these issues, but a part still does. The difficulty for new teachers is understanding that they are not trying to help a child who is a problem. Rather, they are trying to adjust an educational environment that is not serving a child. The student is letting us know, by acting in unacceptable ways, that the environment is not serving his or her needs. Too bad the child cannot just say, "You know, Teacher, how you are teaching is not really connecting with me as an individual. So please reconsider your teaching strategies and your attitudes." Until we help children learn to express themselves more directly, it falls on teachers to figure it out.

THE GOOD ENOUGH TEACHER

Gathering skills for establishing boundaries is integral to humanistic teaching in the classroom. From this vantage, a teacher is working on the development of teaching skills that tap both personal strengths and the desire to do more than transmit information to students. It is not about fulfilling some theoretical image or ideal of the humanistic teacher, but rather the bringing together of the different strands of what make up the whole of the teacher self. And even so, it is much more about engaging in a process, not an achievement—a self that is constantly changing and growing. Staff development that does this kind of training supports the process. It can be a great boon, yet it is not the only path. Collaboration of some sort might be an equal boon. Usually, there is more difficulty entailed in learning these skills on one's own. No matter, teachers are responsible to their students, let alone to themselves, to figure out how to maintain appropriate boundaries in the classroom in a lively and joyful manner. It is likely that any teacher who is engaged in taking on this responsibility is a good enough teacher. There are a lot of ways to count success in regard to the students and oneself.

In the following letter to Dylan, his grandfather, Jerry, shares a few stories about what it was like when he was in school as a student, and later, as a beginning teacher. We have introduced the letter with this short discussion of the good enough teacher, because Jerry rarely felt this way in the classroom for many years after he began teaching. He did consider himself a good enough student but in his own peculiar fashion:

Dear Dylan,

My memories of elementary school are sparse—and nonexistent before I was in third or fourth grade. Even then, I have only images of the classrooms, the school, and a few times I was in the limelight. Born in Milwaukee in 1936, my family moved six years later to Chicago soon after the United States entered into World War II. You would imagine that school would have been a big deal for me, but the truth is I was pretty much oblivious to its relevance in my life. It was something children do, and at best, I felt like an oddball. I didn't care about what we were learning, but I was practical enough to do the work, not misbehave too much, and get decent grades. School didn't ruffle me, except that I didn't like playground games, particularly those that had the potential of violence. Though I must say that playing marbles with other children sticks in my mind as a fun time.

One distinct memory is coming back to school after being out sick for a few days, when I was about nine or ten. While in bed, I had been playing with numbers in connection with drawing geometric shapes. As a result, in my mind, I had discovered a constant between 1 and 2, not unlike pi. I shared the discovery with my teacher, and she said something like "that's interesting." That was the end of the discussion. I'd love to tell you what I actually discovered, but soon after I was on to other adventures and forgot. At the time, I was disappointed, but chalked it up to how little could be expected from being in school.

To be fair, I have to add that in seventh grade my school required all students to take home economics, girls and boys together. I loved the electricity experiments, learning how to fix toilets, baking, and sewing. I still remember what I learned, but most of my memorable learning was done outside of school with friends or on my own. I liked playing with trains, puppets, and magic tricks. I did appreciate that my teachers let me put on a puppet or magic show once in awhile. I also loved going to the Museum of Science and Industry with my friends. My most fun memory is stringing tin can telephone lines between our houses off the back porches.

When the war was over, we moved to Wooddale, a small town of 800 people, 20 miles west of Chicago's Lake Michigan shore. Schools were crowded then, and my eighth-grade class met only for a half day in the morning. Now in the country, my new friends and I had plenty of time to play along the creek and tramp through open fields and the small forest that bordered the town. When I entered high school in the next town over, though, my mother and father made it clear that I was bound for college. Still, I made sure to choose a few classes in woodshop, metalworking, and drafting. And, I took up playing trumpet in the concert band—making sure to practice at least two hours every day. As you can tell, while growing up my education mostly took place outside of the regular classrooms.

What helped to keep me on a college track was the time I spent with friends from Hebrew school and the religious youth group I attended at a synagogue in Chicago several times a week. More significant yet, your sneaky great-grandmother got me a job when I was fifteen as a dishwasher at Camp Ramah, a Hebrew-speaking summer camp in northern Wisconsin. This led over the coming summers to involvement as a camper and a counselor. The teachers and rabbis I met at Ramah steered my friends and me to apply to the University of Chicago when we finished high school. Along with several of them, I attended the university from 1953 until 1962, earning the excessive number of four degrees, including a Ph.D. in educational psychology. What I came there with was concern for making the world a better place to live. What I left with was an idealistic belief that I could meet the needs of every student I would teach. Years later, as you know, I took up trumpet playing again, but not until educating teachers became the core of my life work.

Unlike your grandmother, my mind wasn't on teaching while I was growing up. I did become a part-time teacher while going to college and graduate school, but mainly to earn money for school. I liked teaching, but the problem was that I wasn't very good at it. It wasn't about a lack of knowing the subject matter. I knew what I had to teach. But, I so much wanted to bring the spirit of my childhood learning to the classroom and had only a few clues about how to do this. I was so sure that every student deserved opportunities like those that had engaged me as a child and an adolescent. In contrast, I knew so little about the practice of teaching. All I seemed to know was that I didn't want to teach the way I was taught—leaving me dependent a lot on my sincerity. Helpfully, it turned out to be fairly valuable coin for helping an untrained and unnatural novice survive.

From my childhood and from reading Dewey's Experience and Education early on as a university student, I at least had a clue about good teaching. I always appreciated learning activities that involved practical experience, and this was one of Dewey's major points. So, all the years that I was teaching Hebrew school, tutoring kids in regular school, and being a counselor at a day camp in Chicago, I invented activities and managed, though barely sometimes, to hold my students' interest. Then I graduated from the university, and I was offered a teaching position at Miami University in the Department of Educational Psychology. Somehow I imagined that I could teach college courses well enough with just a text and my clever interpretations and discussion. The first time I taught was a disaster. The fact that my students didn't notice made it worse. A three-hour evening course turned into a long lecture. To make matters worse, I didn't even have a knack for engaging the students in a discussion. Silence confronted my meager efforts, and I had no activities up my sleeve. I had promised myself I wouldn't teach the way I was taught, and there I was endlessly lecturing just like I had been lectured to throughout my education.

The Jewish holidays began the next night, and I wasn't holding class again until the following week. When the students and I met the second time, they were confronted with a slightly crazed teacher who had stayed up late for several nights planning a couple of activities for teaching educational psychology. Like first waffles, they didn't work too well, but they got some discussion going. Without a clear set of boundaries however, there was an up and down level of chaos that occurred and continued throughout the semester. Over the years, as I learned more about myself, my strengths, and more about how meeting the variety of students' needs is feasible, the level of chaos diminished and has almost disappeared. I say almost, because whenever

I try something new as a teacher, I always risk some confusion, resistance, and plain unwillingness to cooperate. The good news is that, although my sincerity is still appreciated by my students, it is more satisfying to depend on our developing respectful relationships with each other.

Love, Grangran

II

A Historical and Personal Context

Educational history over the course of the twentieth century reveals how integral humanistic teaching has been for schooling children. In the early years, Dewey's influence was the predominant factor in the growth of the widespread Progressive Education Association. By mid-century, when our teaching careers began, the consistent shifts that had occurred in how elementary and secondary schools functioned were not difficult to recognize. There were more radical changes in the 1960s, and though many of these have been left behind, the overall influence has been the basis of the continued growth and development of humanistic elements in education ever since. The knowledge that has accumulated, both theoretical and practical, combined with the stories of how we became humanistic teachers, supports our contention that every teacher today has the potential for the meaningful practice of humanistic teaching to some degree.

As a theoretician and a practitioner working together, we enjoyed the opportunities to enlarge this knowledge and apply it to teaching students of all ages. There has been a lively dialogue among us along the way and with many others—where the interaction of theory and practice has had an impact in both directions. Our successes derived from a sensitivity to different kinds of knowledge, including that derived from history, personal experience, young students, emerging teachers, parents, those more experienced than us, and the rest of the stakeholders. The integration informed theory and practice as they continue to inform each other. This collaborative conversation still enriches our teaching every day.

- Remind yourself of memorable moments, good or bad, as a student.
- Organize a few thoughts about the history of education. If not from reading, construct what you heard from your parents and grandparents.
- Frame a brief theory of the *humanistic teacher*, whether or not you believe it is your view. As it were, try it on.
- Take time to discuss with a colleague your reading, the memories, the history, the theory, and examples from your teaching experiences.

3

Student Needs

Most teachers, from our experience, think of themselves as humanistic in some ways. This means that teachers hope to provide the kind of guidance that will help each individual student get the education he or she deserves—in ways that are challenging, supportive, and caring. Spanning conservatives to radicals, some will want their students to follow a path that they believe is right, some will look forward to their students' developing themselves within the broad image of our culture as handed down, and others, like the authors, envision an education that prepares for the unpredictable future as it unfolds—with other possibilities and combinations included. We share idealism as teachers, though, and the hope to reach, and meet the needs of, most every student. There are times when the vision fades, or even disappears in a haze of disappointment. But whenever there is a glimpse, the belief is likely to arise that some of the dream can be fulfilled. In a song sung by Bob the Builder and Wendy, master builders for tiny tots, along with the other characters and all the talking machines, they ask, "Can we do it?!" And with gusto, they answer, "Yes, we can!!" The singing represents everyone's feeling of agency.

MANIFESTO

Maintaining agency, the sense of having the power to act, in the face of difficult, complex, and even intractable obstacles is the problem that got us talking and thinking. Agency is a necessary ingredient for working toward fulfilling a vision. We asked what maintains this sense in the face of setbacks and failures? The vision is that teachers can find successful ways of continuing to act on their ideals without being stopped dead in their tracks. We know that, at times, there are internal psychological pressures that are carried by unwarranted assumptions about our abilities to continue trying. These are assumptions built up from the past that we carry inside our thoughts and feelings, often untrue, yet they become self-fulfilling. Other pressures stem from what the people in charge and the culture at large insist. The bosses. At worst, there is the notion that any kind of humanistic education borders on evil, and at best, there is recognition that the heart wishes it could be so, if it weren't so darn impractical. And, students so often don't cooperate in ways we think they should for their success and ours.

Plus, there is a lot more to think about than student needs, and yes, probably every teacher believes that the individual needs of students should be factored in, but what is so helpful about beginning with them? How does this priority make practical sense? Isn't what children should learn at the least just as important? Yes and no. Most children can be compelled to learn almost anything, even forced under the threat of punishment. But, we are discussing an *effective* education. This is an education where students are likely to remember what they learn, in many ways never forgetting what they have learned. And, it is an education where much more is learned than what we count as remembered; knowing how to solve problems, an ability to express creativity, a passion for learning, and an interest in addressing social and ethical issues are all part of the mix.

The essence of a humanistic education is an obligation to pay attention to the needs of students before considering the ideas that guide an educational program—in ways that lead to achieving these ends. Doing so, however, introduces a way of teaching that has its own brand of problems. In a recent text (Fielstein and Phelps, 2001, p. 53), a teacher who thought this approach could be helpful too quickly dismissed that humanistic teaching leads to chaotic classrooms. It's true that unsuccessful humanistic teaching has many times led to the breakdown of classroom order. This makes a humanistic education an easy target to scapegoat. For the similar reasons that any school program fails to meet the commitments to educate students adequately, it is justifiably criticized. Humanistic education is maligned, though, when the whole of the philosophy is judged in the same breath. What is omitted from the criticism is that teachers are also obligated to figure out, as they would be for any approach to teaching and learning, how to successfully implement their goals. So it was for John Dewey's humanistic theories of education in the early part of the twentieth century—leading him to write a defense. His *Experience and Education*, in 1938, called on common sense, reason, and a deeper understanding of children's needs and how they fit into his progressive, humanistic thinking.

For Dewey, the problem was conceptualized as a matter of progressive versus traditional approaches to education. Looking through two lenses, one personal and the other historical, we notice that humanism is not bound to be progressive in the usual sense. That educators of all stripes desire to be humanistic is not particularly surprising, because the call to educate others has in common concerns about caring about how students will fare in life. But no matter what values a teacher wants to transmit, even inculcate, it has to be admitted that student personalities are all different, just like tastes, fingerprints, and snowflakes. The contexts of their lives vary as much, just as they do for twins growing up together in the same home. All the various people who have a stake in education further influence these contexts. Progressive, traditional, and the stances in-between are most effectively expressed by responding to students' individual needs as learners. It is not a matter of looking backward or forward; rather, a way of expressing real care that all students have a chance to be successful. The challenge is to try; the challenge is to do; the challenge is to be humanistic.

There is an undeniable subversiveness about the argument. Humanistic education normally implies more liberalness than typically abounds in American culture and beyond. But the argument is mostly a practical one on other levels. Even when using rote learning, the teacher has to deal with how students differ. It's long been known that reinforcing learning doesn't work the same for everyone. On another level far removed from this problem, there are few educators who would not want students to realize their potential, however that is interpreted. *What* we learn is determined by the many contexts that have been noted, and they are not generally humanistic in any common sense. *How* we learn, on the other hand, after Dewey's influence, is intrinsically a humanistic issue. It is possible to learn under negative circumstances. Indeed, it is not uncommon. Better yet, we know that highly supportive conditions for learning are optimal; it should be understood without argument. Skills are required that address the variety of experience that one confronts in daily life—now and in the future. It is unhelpful to believe that coping in the future, or the present, can be transformed into a predictable endeavor. In the end, the argument is practical, even as it is idealistic. This is what education should mean.

PERSONAL HISTORY

Altogether, our early education took place in six elementary schools and two high schools, in the Midwest, including schools in large and small cities, and one rural one too. Usually, the buildings were from before World War II, sometimes much older. Bolted down desks were common, inkwells were just going out of fashion, and there were cloakrooms where we could "secretly" create a bit of havoc. It wasn't easy for anyone to argue that schools were essentially joyous places. Indeed, children called them prisons, which wasn't far-fetched. Still, we didn't know there was an alternative to not liking school, and so we went willingly looking for the fun we might have with other children. The two of us did like learning, knew that school would help, but vaguely wondered why we were so miserable.

We wonder what you think about this next letter written to our grandson to read when he is older. It's for him to ponder about what education was like for his grandmother, Donna, when she went to school in the 1940s and 1950s:

Dear Dylan,

Grangran and I decided that I should write a letter to you about my school experiences. You see I became a teacher and then went on to help start a school because my schooling was so very unpleasant for me. I helped start Project Learn because I did not want your momma or Aunt Simone to suffer the same kind of mis-education I did.

One of my first memories and my best memory is walking over one mile to school every day—even when the snow was piled above my head along the sidewalks. We were living in Minneapolis, Minnesota, and everyday, I also walked home for lunch. That was really fun. Part of the way I walked with different schoolmates, but since I lived in another school district, I had to walk about five blocks by myself. I really loved that part of each day—when I was walking alone. I got to know all the dogs on the way home, and once I brought one home with me and asked my momma if we could keep it. She made me take it back to its home and put it back in the fenced yard from which I had liberated it. I loved collecting worms and bugs in cans or boxes. I climbed trees and made up stories.

But when I got to school, all that stopped. I had to go to the girls' playground that was a very small cement square for girls from kindergarten through second grade. In third grade, girls got a bigger playground with swings. But the boys got to play on a great big field (so it looked to me!), plus a big cement playground with swings. I really wanted to play with the boys, because they got to play baseball and the girls didn't. We had to line up to go inside and were not allowed to speak once we lined up. We were not allowed to speak once we were in school unless we raised our hands and were given permission. This confused me because the teachers told us regularly that we should be learning to cooperate with one another. I couldn't figure out how we could do this when we were not allowed to talk to one another. It was very hard for me to be "good" when I was in school. I had a hard time not talking to my friends so I got into trouble, sort of . . . well really, I think I was quite a good girl and a good student. The teachers said that I just had too much energy—like the boys.

I don't remember that my teachers were really mean, but they weren't very nice. They seemed to like the children who were quiet, neat, and good spellers. I was none of those things. I had a particular problem with pencils. I chewed them, and somehow I always chewed the erasers off the pencils. And, my teachers would embarrass me in front of all the other children for this "disgusting" habit. I really tried hard not to chew on my pencils, but somehow I just couldn't stop.

The teachers made it clear that the good children would get the special treats, and the others would know they just weren't good enough. I wanted so badly to take notes to the office and to other teacher's rooms or to be chosen to pass out the milk and cookies at snack time. One time, I was chosen for a very special treat, but it cost me so much shame that I am not sure it was worth being chosen. The teacher had ten tickets for a play at the University of Minnesota's Children's Theatre and there were forty-five children in my fourth-grade class. She said she was choosing the best boys and girls as a reward to them for being so good. She called out nine names and with each name I was so disappointed. Before she said the tenth name, she told the class that the tenth person was not a good girl but because she was such a talented girl, the teacher was making an exception and sending her to the play with the good children. She then called my name. I was both excited and so ashamed. As much as I wanted to go to the play, I really wanted to be one of the good children.

My school in Minneapolis was a very large old dark brick building. The halls were dark, and the windows in the rooms were way high . . . for a little kid . . . and they were opened with a long pole from the top. The desks were bolted to the floor. Some had tops that lifted up so I could put my books and papers and pencils inside. My desk was messy and the teachers didn't like that at all.

Once we came into the room, we sat in the desk assigned to us and stayed there the rest of the day—except for recess and lunch.

We did not move around without permission from the teacher—even to sharpen a pencil. We all had to line up to go to the bathroom, girls one time, boys another. I think we were able to get up and get a book to read if we finished our work, but I'm not sure.

It was very hard for me to be in school, very hard. I had no trouble learning the things the teacher wanted me to learn. In fact, I did very, very well in all my schoolwork except for spelling and handwriting, and that seemed to me what my teachers thought were the two most important subjects in the school curriculum. My stories were not posted because they were not the neatest papers. They may have been the best stories, but that didn't seem to be important.

It was hard for me to go back to school after lunch. I so much wanted to go outside and play in the park across the street from my house and find tadpoles in the creek and frogs on the bank. I liked to dig in the mud and build mud houses for the frogs that never, ever went into the houses I built for them. But I was dutiful and returned to school. The afternoons were even harder than the mornings . . . they seemed to drag on and on. I know some of my teachers tried very hard to make school interesting. I remember Mrs. Ziggafoose, the third-grade teacher who would cook starch in a big kettle and give a big glob of it to each child at her desk along with another glob—of paint, which we mixed together to make a finger painting. We did this at the end of the day so the paintings would dry on our desks by the next day. It was very courageous of her, and I liked making those paintings. And, she did it more than once during the year . . . a very brave woman. A funny thing about Mrs. Ziggafoose is that when I moved to Ames, Iowa, in fifth grade, her nephew, Dick Ziggafoose, was in my class. I kind of liked Mrs. Ziggafoose even if she did like the other girls who were tidier than me.

In second grade, we made class murals of the different seasons. I still have a class picture, which has a bit of the winter mural in it. Everyone would draw something that might be part of the mural, and then the teacher would select the best ones to be in the class mural. My picture of a girl ice-skating was chosen. But not everyone got to be chosen. There were over 39 children in my second-grade class, and just a few of them made pictures that were good enough to be part of the mural.

The school building in Ames was a bit lighter than the one in Minneapolis. And the girls could play on the big playground there. There were still a little kids' playground and a big kids' playground, but not separated by boys and girls.

Much of my life in school from fifth grade on still involved trying to be chosen by my teachers. I had a lot of friends and I did feel chosen by them, but school continued to be a trial for me. My new school went through ninth grade even though ninth grade was considered part of high school by the state of Iowa. I continued to do very well in my subjects. I got 95 or higher in first-year Latin and that was an A. There were teachers, Mrs. Coulter was one, who gave me B's because I was such a poor speller and had poor handwriting. When I graduated from the University of Iowa with honors and Phi Beta Kappa, Mrs. Coulter said to me that she was surprised. She never believed I could do so well. I guess that sort of summarizes my sense of what my education was like. My teachers didn't know me or what I was capable of. They only knew what they expected, not what I needed or wanted. I seemed to be irrelevant to them in the scheme of things that was education, particularly in Ames in the 1950s.

There were a few important parts of my high school education that related to my interests and me. I was on the debate and discussion team, which went around the state and debated other high school teams. I was part of the school theater involved in plays and productions and was elected to the theater honor group when I was a junior in high school. Very few folks got into that group before they were seniors. My theater and debate teacher did like me and seemed to know something of who I was.

My best teacher ever was my high school chemistry teacher, Mr. Trump. He was a very serious, dour man who rarely smiled, but oh did he make chemistry interesting and relevant to me. The first day in the class, he demonstrated how when you put a drop of clear phenolphthalein into a beaker of clear liquid acid, the compound turned red. For me this was magic. I must have looked so amazed. How did two clear liquids turn red? Where did the red come from? My teacher brought the beakers to my table and told me that I could do it myself. He then let me add another clear liquid that took the red away. That teacher knew who I was and what I needed. I loved chemistry from that minute on and literally would run down the hall to his class.

As I got older, I did experience a great deal more recognition from my teachers and professors. They thought I was very smart and an exceptional student, but still I never really felt like they knew me or that my education related very much to me, not until I was in graduate school at Temple University. There, I did feel the connection between what I was learning and who I am.

Love, Nana

The stories we've shared with each other, for nearly fifty years, from our separate pasts may have changed some over time, but they have consistently supported an all-encompassing story that we simply didn't like school. Mainly, we have concluded that our needs as students received too little attention. We believe that this began in kindergarten and continued on through college. Our conclusion has not wavered, but the picture has enlarged. Something more than drab color has appeared. From examining the new picture, we notice that the dislike is less figural than the intriguing details of what we remember and what it was we did like. Certainly, not everyone has the strong negative feelings on which we base our thinking, and there are those who really enjoyed going to school. Still, there is something to learn from understanding the fullness of past experience—as a path toward making education less imperfect.

Identifying missing elements raised new questions. Helpful subtleties appeared, affirming that there is more to reinventing education than just trying to be different from the present reality. It was pleasantly surprising that our reflection led to a more complex image of the vision we have held for so long. What we are looking for are changes, maybe just small shifts that have the potential for moving away from the status quo to a more relevant and lively education for students today and tomorrow. It is something all teachers want, and for us it begins with figuring out how to address the needs of every student even in a traditional setting.

HISTORICAL CONTEXT

As students, like most others, we weren't concerned with a historical context. This larger picture probably was not on the mind of our teachers either. Though they were likely to have taken courses in the history of education as part of their preparation for teaching, getting the tasks of the everyday job of managing the classroom done had to be figural. Without a wider perspective, they were unlikely to see what was in the background that is more visible now.

The year 1950, at half century, was a good marking point for strengthening one's belief in the American dream. If the era around this year had a theme, it was agency. The planet had survived World War II, the wonders of science abounded, and there was plenty of optimism in the air. It was a time to imagine the realistic possibility of creating a more perfect world. Obstacles were abundant too, including intractable ones, but the mood was essentially unaffected by them. Even a discouraged teacher would have been much less gloomy than we were as students, and it was more likely that many teachers were excited about the potential of education for transforming society and guiding children in ways that could well benefit them in the world of their future.

Paradoxically, this was when the Progressive Education Association was dying, indeed demised by the mid-1950s. It wasn't long before Lawrence Cremin (1961) offered a positive interpretation: "granted the collapse of progressive education as an organized movement, there remained a timelessness about many of the problems the progressives raised and the solutions they proposed" (p. 352). The philosophy had its beginnings in the late 1800s; because of its ongoing success, without difficulty a national association was formed in the winter of 1918–1919. Over the next three decades, the influence of progressive education continued to expand. But by 1950, so much of Dewey's philosophy had affected teaching and learning in U.S. schools, it was no longer necessary to join a radical group to benefit from the fruits of those who had done the pioneering. For Cremin, "progressive education had become the conventional wisdom of the fifties" (p. 352). This meant that schools included programs that were designed to improve health, prepare for an occupation, and care for the quality of family and community life. The focus of education included significant attention to children of different interests and abilities. The aims of progressive education stood for a free and full development of each individual child, and this attitude toward education had quite thoroughly imbued the culture of U.S. schools.

What makes the picture larger yet, and more complex, was an overlay of a new set of compelling concepts that were being introduced. There were futuristic concepts along with practical ideas for classroom teaching emerging from academic research that promised near perfect ways of helping children learn. Many of them centered around theories of behaviorism primarily based on experiments involving animal conditioning. Great advances in this research had been made during the war, boosting the name of B. F. Skinner to prominence—whose name in a few years would represent a competitive and contentious match for the reputation of John Dewey (Spring, 1997). Skinner's reinforcement theories might have been modestly introduced as interesting variations on how children's learning can be facilitated, let alone all human learning and every species of the animal kingdom; rather, it was accompanied by a promise, science fiction in scope, that it was the best and only way to truly help children learn. And in terms of students' individual needs, it looked good, for it seemed every student could learn at his or her pace. What got lost was the possibility that children learn in very different ways, thus ignoring how this vision was a serious move back toward square one and a drabber picture.

The optimistic mood of this era would have been better supported by the humanistic developments that had taken place in

U.S. schools since the turn of the twentieth century, many of them profound. Over fifty years, there had been a gradual "shift away from a narrow focus on the content of schooling . . . toward an emphasis on students as persons" (Allender, 1982, p. 94). The troubled mix of humanism with its overlay of behaviorism diluted the progress of progressive education by functionally masking its impact. The shift had made schools more democratic—a significant element of the American dream. Moreover, the progressive philosophical concepts had become embodied in the practical everyday practice of teaching. What was missing was an active awareness of this history, which would have given teachers a more realistic understanding of agency. Yet, a transformation in American schooling had already occurred.

We can also see that neither the magnitude of the scientific promises nor the breadth of the progressive changes seemed to have touched the two of us when we were in school back then. Many factors account for this. To be sure, what's left out of history are the daily frustrations that teachers and students experience in their efforts to achieve their own individual and idiosyncratic goals. History informs us of what happened in general but not how it affected teachers or the students who were the living characters in the story. That the promises didn't contribute at least some likeable novelty in our education is the easiest to understand. They hadn't yet become so popular that they would have reached many schools. It was mainly the idea of them that created a hope, one that in the final analysis couldn't realistically be fulfilled anyway. Maybe this futuristic hope created a cloud that made it difficult to see accomplishments in hand. Managing daily frustrations can make a teacher yearn for better methods of teaching. Seeing oneself deprived of the promise is frustrating.

Even so, what remains is a poignant question: why didn't significant effects of progressive education show up in Donna's elementary school? Dewey and Skinner were not the whole story. Other historical details show how in many ways we were actually, directly and indirectly, affected and nurtured by our schooling. Around the time we were born, Frank Graves (1936), in a section entitled, "Recent Tendencies in American Education," discussed what he considered an extensive range of progressive changes that were presently occurring. Reading Graves, we see the beginnings of industrial and commercial training, agricultural education, and home economics. As well, there are programs for the handicapped, nursery schools, junior high schools for preteens, adult education, and junior colleges. Attention was being given to ability grouping and individual adjustment, and there were other experimental progressive programs, in addition to those based on Dewey's philosophies, particularly those that stemmed from observations about child development. These were all actively developing programs aimed at making schools more inclusive. The meaning of schooling was broadening under an umbrella of widespread enthusiasm for progressive education all around.

This expanded conception of schooling addressed itself to a variety of stakeholders, initiating a long-lasting presence of the new programs, most of them permanently, within the institution of education. So certainly, these developments were a part of how school affected the two of us—to our benefit. There can be little question that the kind of education we did receive in large measure accounts for how well we learned to cope; we have to recognize its central contribution to how we learned to function, at least, intellectually. Questioning what was missing, therefore, becomes more complex.

By recalling our personal educational history, we brought to mind the absence of attention to our needs as students. As our concerns become more articulate, we worry that students, then and still, are excluded from their share of power, reserved for all other stakeholders, in their own education. It is a familiar argument that students can't know what they need, but there is a flaw in this argument. The ideas that are used to develop an educational program, subject matter and process, are certainly the province of teachers and other adults who have a stake in them. But, no one person should dictate the nature of the educational programs nor should any single group of stakeholders. All parties who are involved should be provided with opportunities, with the hope of having an impact on what emerges. The planning does begin with educators tapping their knowledge about how children of all ages learn and formulating curriculum based on adult values. It might or might not include the input of students. But carrying out the plans depends on continuous listening and responding to the needs of students.

Dewey (1900) fundamentally, if not particularly, understood this requirement at the beginning of the twentieth century: "Abandon the notion of subject-matter as something fixed and ready-made in itself, outside the child's experience; cease thinking of the child's experience as also something hard and fast; see it as something fluent, embryonic, vital; and we realize that the child and the curriculum are simply two limits which define a single process." Adding, "it is continuous reconstruction, moving from the child's present experience out into that represented by the organized bodies of truth that we call studies" (p. 189).

No doubt, progressivism is a many-faceted concept. Cremin noted, "The movement was marked from the very beginning by a pluralistic, frequently contradictory, character. The reader will search in vain for any capsule definition" (1961, p. x). But, with Dewey's support, we are hoping that the concept of students as primary stakeholders, *in the process of being educated,* is underscored as central in response to the challenge for teachers to be humanistic.

From Graves's (1936) view, humanistic kinds of education trace back to the Renaissance. At that point in history, there was little or no connection to the process of education. Importantly, there was a "revival of learning," much of it bringing to the present the Greek and Latin classics from the distant past. An absence of ancient literature was felt; a need to expand beyond the bounds of religious scholarship came into the light. Clearly, the focus wasn't on the potential of the individual as much as it was on reconceptualizing the nature of knowledge. Furthermore, it was all about higher learning; though, the limited founding of grammar schools foreshadowed the future of education. More significantly, the expansion of personal knowledge signaled what was humanistic. In the evolution of the concept of humanistic education, there grew a greater understanding of the needs of students and the importance of attending to educational process.

The history of education, unlike general history that so often catalogs the gory details of human conflicts, is more about triumphs, with few lasting regrets, in a long story of success. From the time of the Renaissance till 1936, when Graves completed *A Student's History of Education,* there is a grand sense of progress—progressivism in an array of accomplishments. And, so it was for Cubberley in 1919 when he completed *Public Education in the United States.* He marveled how the first fifty years since the founding of his nation brought, once again, a transition from church-controlled education to the birth of education fully supported by the "state." And when the final chapter reaches the year in which he was writing, he enthusiastically concluded, "The schools have been made free and equally open to all . . . [and] a thoroughly democratic educational ladder has everywhere been provided" (p. 495).

Almost the same pattern was found in Joel Spring (1997); chapter after chapter mirrored the list that Graves (1936) used to summarize the progress of education earlier in the century. There was, however, a telling shift in the last chapter. The end of the twentieth century was marked by a description of strident conservatism that put U.S. education in retrograde. Contrary to the mood we have found in other education history books, we wondered why? Maybe the times were truly tougher, as they still seem to be. His last chapter brought to mind Donna's letter to Dylan. As well, it brought to mind the education text that accused humanistic education as being typically chaotic. As we have said, though, when too close in time to the daily job of teaching and learning, it's hard to see the trail of triumph. Graves (1913) in an earlier book better captured the big picture, with ideas that may directly reflect the influence of John Dewey: "Thus the central problem in education of the twentieth and succeeding centuries is to be a constant reconstruction of the curriculum and methods of teaching so as to harmonize a due regard for the progressive variations of the individual with the welfare of the conservative institutions of society" (pp. 402–403).

There will always be tensions between the needs of the individual and the goals of society—a confusing jumble of so many individuals and so many goals. Our experience and research over the last fifty years, working together as educators in many roles, argues for addressing these tensions by giving priority to the needs of students. The overwhelming problems of educating children, and ourselves, will never disappear. However, our vision is aimed at actually making problems less intractable. Life's lesson: we do the job, and hope over the long haul, we do some good. This is the best we'll get.

WHO UNBOLTED THE SCHOOL DESKS?

Sitting at dinner one night talking about writing this book, Ed Kiess, a long-time friend, wondered, who unbolted the desks from the classroom floor? The question was intriguing, particularly from someone who has been a classroom teacher, principal, and superintendent, now retired and, as we are, still involved in education. We had all sat at these desks, yet they disappeared by the time we had become teachers in the late 1950s. We knew of one case in New York City of a design for rows of bolted desks—48 through grades 4, 45 up to grade 6, and 40 for grades 7 and 8. The design was attributed to a New York school and classroom architect with the intent to avoid noise and confusion (Spring, 1997). There was no discussion about how they got unbolted, all within the first half of the twentieth century.

Whatever the answer, probably there was a string of influences that led to requisitioning the custodian to give the desks their freedom. The absence of common knowledge about the fate of bolted desks illustrates the possibility and potential of uncontested rebellions. For a teacher, or any other educator in the system, to turn ideas—about thinking and acting more humanistically in the classroom—into practice requires risking rebellion of some kind. It might be done quietly, just asking, or with a bit of complaining, trying some politics, ignoring a request, enlisting a few conspirators, or maybe something bolder. Humor helps, because the underlying goal is to maintain vitality without losing one's job. Some of these rebellions succeed, some do not. Making an effort to maintain good relationships with one's peers and superiors is also on the list, but it doesn't negate turning ideas into practice by turning people around in the effort.

Sometimes, it can be easy. Donna's chemistry teacher, the one she wrote about in her letter to Dylan, took less than 15 minutes to transform her into an avid chemistry student. It took only a little effort on the part of the teacher, yet it meant a great deal. As well, she remembers that this happened for other students in class. They too were stimulated and excited. Even if her memory is exaggerated, the reputation of this teacher was built on how he paid attention to each of his students, touching at least some of them with the magic that they needed. Typically, he would have simply been called a great teacher. You wouldn't think to call him rebellious, because his rebellion was so quiet. It is a risk, though, to take time from covering more chemistry and to leave time for getting to know students better, thus increasing the chance that what they do end up learning is even greater than if their noses were kept to the grindstone.

What if other teachers, especially when Donna was little, were to have expressed an interest in who she was—had inquired about her thoughts, feelings, and experiences? What an amazing thing it would have been if her kindergarten teacher had asked her to talk about walking to and from school, then wanted the worms she collected to put in an aquarium with dirt to watch what worms do. What a thought! How different school might have been.

But not every teacher is able to take that time. Too often, the magnitude of the problems we face leaves us discouraged; creative ideas about teaching are so distant and out of reach, we do only what we can to survive. Not only are student needs not met, neither are those of the teachers. We're all important, but when the central characters in the story are given short shrift, everybody loses. When demands are conflicting, apparently insurmountable problems arise. Their intractability is essentially the inability to get outside the box of stakeholders pulling in different, often opposite, directions. But, if at the least our students could be brought into a partnership, working with each other and the teacher in mutually supportive relationships, so much of the immediate confusion of a classroom would be diminished—without bolting down the desks.

The practical answer for teachers lies in small creative moves that shift confrontations off the course of a head-on collision in order to better meet students' needs. If necessary, the place to begin is with students' misbehavior. There are so many kinds—including the possibility of physical violence—that the universe seems to have more than four dimensions (including time in the count). The immediacy of the conflicts breeds intractability, and there are out-of-control situations where resolution is beyond the classroom. In general, we can't discount serious problems that lay outside the power of small shifts. Adding to the list are unreasonable pressures for children to pass mandated tests, the absence of adequate materials, the lack of support from colleagues and superiors, pressures to complete excessive administrative detail, difficult or devastating multicultural tensions, and other overwhelming stressors. Furthermore, the full picture undermines any sense of agency. Having said this, why bother trying? How can one imagine making a difference is possible? Where conceivably in all of this fits the challenge to be humanistic? A manifesto, personal histories, and a historical context are senseless if they are not followed by how these ideas can be translated into practice. The question is not new: what do we do on Monday?

There are few immediate solutions to most of these problems, but there remains potential for those that can be eased by attention to student needs. It's about talking, about conversation. When the problems are about classroom management, talking is usually the most effective place to begin after stopping physical harm from occurring by any feasible means. And, the strategy is the same for those wishes that would bring about a great class to teach. At whatever level we enter into the problem of not meeting student needs, it's essentially the conversations in which we engage students that make the difference—that constitute the small moves that open the possibility for change that is more immediately within the teacher's control. They are within reach of a vision that the learning environment can be different now, within reach of a sense of agency that the vision creates, and within reach of meaningful impact that appears to be a bit of the magic. If the problems are about classroom behavior, the teacher must figure out how students' needs most effectively impact on their willingness to enter into a mutually supportive relationship with the teacher and the other students.

We ask students, particularly children, to work together—in face of the fact that they are required not to talk to each other most of the time. Even when classes include many opportunities for discussion, it's about the subject. Teachers have the power to engage their students in discussions about how their needs are being met. These discussions can include the whole class. They can be in small groups, without the direct influence of the teacher, where the students learn to participate in a democratic society. They can be individually with the teacher. All this takes time, and it's not an issue of giving up on the many other demands that exist in every classroom. What's at issue is giving some of the time to the process of tapping the needs, which every individual should have opportunities to express. We search for possible ways that these needs might be met within the confines of what might be possible. "We can't always get what we want," to reframe the song by the Rolling Stones, "but if we try sometime, we get what we need." To live in less of a world than this is to shortchange our children and ourselves.

We have the power to browbeat students of all ages into submission. The consequences of this behavior have at times been visibly ugly, frightening, and in the extreme, deadly. As to the rest of the stakeholders, it is maximally disturbing when the most fervent turn out to be the least moral. Education can never succeed at helping people to become good democratic citizens by simply inculcating work skills and moral values. Agency, with the hope of an impact that blesses one's own life and that of others, is necessary, and it requires thoughtful conversation, where there is the opportunity to participate in discussing one's needs and the needs of the community. Teachers begin by acting as a model for their students. We discover our own agency as we help others discover theirs. The challenge to be humanistic is answered by working toward mutually supportive relationships with students so that they will learn most effectively all that they need to learn—by our standards and theirs in relationship. The word *relationship* is key in a more humanistic world. Another last word: it is likely that the noise levels in classrooms will not be decreased.

4

Teacher Needs

Too many teachers spend too much time feeling badly. It's one thing to think of oneself as humanistic in some ways and another to find the energy to expand this belief into an idealistic philosophy of education—even if the involvement is only small shifts in the daily work of teaching. There is so much else going on that has to be juggled; there are so many competing demands from the stakeholders and from one's own expectations as well. Needs! Start out with making sure that there is a life outside of school that gives a chance of being a happy teacher inside the building. It's a tough call to decide how much of one's time will be devoted to being the best teacher possible. Movie images, book characters, real-life people who are held up as supermodels, and our ideals all call for more time than we have, let alone may choose to offer. Then, how much support we can expect to get from other teachers, the principal, other administrators, parents, and family has to be realistic. Besides, there is the regular extra burden of administrative details and the occasional battles that sap energy. Add the fears that students are often uncooperative and sometimes out of control. Even with a group of eager students, there is the multitude of problems that their unmet needs bring to the classroom. It must rankle to suggest that students' needs have to come first.

TAKING RISKS

Teaching, much like the rest of life, is about finding ways to meet our needs so that we do better than survive, hopefully managing to enjoy our work, and in the case of teaching, finding practical opportunities to express some of the idealism in our hearts. Not infrequently the image of a seesaw fits the day-to-day life of the classroom. The distance between enthusiasm and feeling discouraged is not far. Here, though, in the space in-between is where unreachable fantasies are separated from palpable degrees of empowerment. In this space, it is possible to get a little closer to ideals with small changes that lie within the grasp of our own doing. Working toward solving major problems is always part of what has to be done; yet their solution might not be reached even within a lifetime of teaching. And, there are times when daily teaching is so close to survival that it is not possible to imagine a few creative risks. One can only hope for moments when a window opens. In general, though, it's a matter of finding a bit of room to maneuver.

The picture is daunting, and the academic standards that define teachers' goals have yet to be mentioned. There is no success if students don't learn a good deal of what a teacher sets out to teach. In our favor, though there are too many outside tests administered, a great deal still hinges on a teacher's decisions concerning how to facilitate classroom work. There is the possibility of realizing not only the standards set by outsiders but also one's personal goals in the bargain. Even in the shadow of ubiquitous testing, the classroom is still the major place where students acquire knowledge and develop skills.

It is a matter of risk. To find a better match with students' needs, there is usually some room for modifying the standards themselves, certainly the personal ones; and there is even more room for reconsidering teaching strategies. On beyond rote learning, there are other options like students finding facts on their own, focusing on problem solving skills that connect the facts, encouraging students to guide large elements of their own learning, or banking on a basic trust of children's inquiry skills when they work independently in small groups. Anyone of them might result in equal or better student achievement. For sure, most of these options are unlikely to be within reach of students who are floundering. It is the conversations with students that help the teacher decide on what to offer, what to encourage, and what to expect. Ideals are kept in sight; students too are buoyed by the prospect of challenging new options. It's a matter of choosing, more than the level of risk, the kinds to take. The process defines the style of teaching that will be used to meet the students' needs while meeting one's own. Of course, there are no guarantees, a fact which is always true, no matter how we teach. It's more about being practical than idealistic.

Sticking to ideals, there is the peculiar tendency to view human-istic efforts as an all or nothing proposition. The worst example we've seen many times, ludicrous as it should seem, is to instruct students that they can choose to do what they want, and to con-clude when various degrees of chaos erupt, that they are not ready for this responsibility. We agree. Moreover, it is not just extreme examples that are of issue. However we might try to humanize our teaching, we can easily take missteps that don't succeed in ways we imagined. In the larger picture, humanistic teaching is not about free choice so much as it is about conversations that reveal students' needs, which guide us toward responsive teaching.

Most often, students appreciate closer involvement and partici-pation in some of the decisions that a teacher makes each day. This participation is what creates a sense of freedom; and its meaning for the learner is more intrinsically profound than it appears on the surface. There is no place for students to control the basic dimen-sions that define the teaching of any course of study. In a typical adult democracy, representatives are elected to create and provide leadership for setting rules, responsibilities, and measures of free-dom under which people will live together in a society. A democratic classroom requires a parallel set of rules and guidelines, and though students can be invited, even elected, to participate in the process, the final say rests with the teacher and the other adults who have power. Fundamentally, governments come and go, but students have to live with the leadership they are provided.

What makes a classroom democratic is meaningful student input, sometimes great, that has a fair chance of affecting the process and product. The input expresses the students' concerns. The task is to integrate this information into the daily activity of teaching. On the one hand, the range of choices is bound to increase for students. On the other, teachers continue to recognize their responsibility for the ultimate success of class endeavors. Students have to do the work that is theirs to do, but none of this will work well unless the whole of it satisfies a full interactive set of the teacher's goals.

With this understanding, we needn't worry that paying attention to students' needs will blindside ourselves from our own. The re-sponsibility of the teacher is to create a learning environment where an effective partnership functions within a class society, yet students and teachers have intrinsically different roles. In an ini-tial glance, it might appear that the emphasis on making sure that teachers find substantial satisfaction negates the assumption that students' needs come first. How can it be that the needs of stu-dents come first? What is masked in the argument is the context within which the student needs will be met. Children sense the context intuitively. They rarely think that they would rather be elsewhere; what they want is *here* to be different. And for older students, the feelings are really much the same. The teacher, in every case, meets the challenge to be humanistic simply by holding the belief that student needs come first—as the best way to achieve his or her goals. There is no paradox, because decisions like these are supposed to be made by the teachers; it is not within the purview of the student role.

Once choices are made, sufficient slack comes with not trying to do it all. Neither all of the student needs will be met, nor will the teacher's goals be achieved at the highest level one might wish. The task is to find ways to fit the sundry needs into a learning environment where many more of them are likely to be met than before. What is happening is not unlike any classroom, or society for that matter. There are lots of needs, many more than there are students, and for sure, a host of problems. Only the angle is different. Teaching from a fresh point of view, in a style that comes closer to meeting one's needs, is what is important. It is a kind of teaching that is as varied as there are teachers. It is an opportunity to grow and learn, to develop the teacher self, by building on the skills and strengths with which we arrived on the job. Student and teacher needs become part of a more harmonious concert, where, with a bit of luck, there is a feeling of being on the same team.

Meeting teacher needs is a search for ways to guide a classroom that coincide with our values, abilities, and style. It is not glib to say that teaching should be mostly fun; a difficult job doesn't preclude enjoying oneself. Besides, the teacher models and sets a standard for the work that students will do. Involving students in what is happening in class usually requires taking on responsibilities of a different nature than they have come to expect. Teachers must tailor lessons to a level that students can handle; students still have to work hard. Harder, some say. Subject matter is always key. Here in addition, students are participants in a teaching and learning process that strives toward mutually supportive relationships.

If all goes well, what compensates for taking these risks is greater achievement and greater teacher and student satisfaction. Success depends on a personal assessment of how well the gamut of the teacher needs have been met. No different than the students, teachers too can fall short. But not challenging ourselves is to admit a failure to meet our responsibility to the students. Nothing has to be grandiose, or catastrophic. Adding up little triumphs for the students and the teacher is most often enough for feeling good about oneself.

THE THEORETICIAN AND
THE PRACTITIONER

Almost as soon as we met, besides falling in love, we began talking about education. Now, nearly fifty years later, this discussion is still a colorful part of our conversations. Jerry was then a graduate student at the University of Chicago, and Donna was a first-year teacher in a small town outside of Chicago. Though we have reversed roles on occasion, it was established early on that he was the better theoretician and she the better teacher. We knew that we valued practical teaching skills more, but recognized that good theory was necessary to meet the ongoing challenge of becoming better teachers. We were also aware that some important things were missing from our education, and we were bound and determined to make a difference. It wouldn't have been possible then to say that students' needs come first—to have articulated the argument as we have done here—but both the theory and the practice functioned along the lines of this assumption. So they say, some marriages are made in heaven; we suspect that a good part of ours was made in the classroom. And as a matter of fact, the day after Jerry proposed, Donna called during her lunch break at school, after thinking it over, to say that she accepted the offer.

We didn't pay much attention to taking care of our teacher needs in a fashion that would reflect what we know now. The network of pressures that have been discussed was not on our minds consciously. As beginning teachers, it was the need to be successful that crowded out everything else. This is what prominently occupied our consciousness. Underneath were doubts about whether what we wanted was doable and on the surface was an inflated sense of agency that came with the times. Doubts were overshadowed by a belief in the power of a mighty effort. Taking risks was synonymous with making the effort. Success had nothing to do with being kept on the job or fired; it was about how well we found multiple paths to meet the needs of every student in class.

As romantic as we were then, this hope still stands after all these years. But now, tempered by enough mistakes to change the meaning of success, we recognize that the effort itself is more important than substantially helping every student. Maybe in the long run, students' feeling appreciated will make a difference to them, but certainly, as it has turned out, an exploration of our failures always provided significant lessons about how to teach differently in the future when similar obstacles would arise. Notwithstanding, the more limited vision we had at the time served to make teaching less complicated, a blessing every new teacher deserves.

Thinking about teaching and learning was a welcome complica-
tion. There was a great outpouring of new theories at the University
of Chicago, built on the foundation of educational research that supported the significant changes that had occurred between 1900 and
mid-century. Broad horizons, before unseen, were opened to view.
These were exciting times, the 1950s and early 1960s, in Judd Hall,
which housed the Department of Education and the Laboratory
School for elementary students, founded in 1896 by husband and
wife, John and Alice Dewey, the director and principal until they left
in 1904. With the school as a living tradition in the building, having
never lost its place on the front edge of educational reform, a vibrant
group of old and new professors carried out their research, proposed
their theories, and offered opportunities to the teachers in the Lab
School, as it was known, and graduate students, to explore practical applications. Another tradition, long since gone, were morning
and afternoon teas served in real china cups with saucers in the
Judd Hall lounge—with faculty and students regularly attending.
The old days weren't better, but they provided a vehicle for dialogue
that carried and sustained the excitement.

Every history is entitled to name its stars, and Joseph Schwab
was one of them. He was a philosophy of education professor whose
teaching focused on understanding the essential functions of inquiry skills. Early on, he was Jerry's professor in the final course
required of all students in the undergraduate college for general
studies. There, the students read, wrote, and thought about the organization, methods, and principles that underlie the creation of
knowledge. In the Department of Education, Schwab's graduate
courses focused inquiry skills on the exploration of teaching and
learning. In his terms, they were essential to organizing any subject matter, from learning how to read or do arithmetic to the study
of art, social studies, and science. This organization had a crucial
role for the design of teaching methods and the integration of educational principles into the facilitation of learning.

Six years later, as a dissertation adviser, he tutored Jerry in the
widest practical everyday meanings of how inquiry skills affect all
learning. It might not be the approach of choice for learning about
the practice of teaching today, but it was the pinnacle of knowledge for the students who were studying education at the University of Chicago in those days. But for teachers, or anyone, the
study of inquiry processes could not be fit into a cookbook for an-
swering questions. Nothing could have been further from Schwab's
mind. This kind of study was a piece of the university's central goal
to mine for knowledge in great fields of the unknown. And for educators at every level, it was meant to put us in charge of finding

our own answers. "Enquiry," as he wrote, "is not a universal method or logic. . . . On the contrary, it is only a generic envelope for a plurality of concrete enquiries" (Schwab, 1962, p. 103). Indeed, plurality abounded. And agency soared, though admittedly, a little too high at times.

Another of the stars was Benjamin Bloom, who was an integral member of the examination committee charged with evaluating the progress of students in the undergraduate college. For this task, he and his colleagues developed *The Taxonomy of Educational Objectives*, still in print and relevant today (Bloom, 1956). Skinnerian theory, so popular then, was stunningly diminished by *The Taxonomy*. In outlining a "cognitive domain" that ranged in ascending order of mental activity, the conception of educational objectives was broadened from nothing more than mastery with rote learning to skills closer to the inquiry skills that Schwab's discussions posed as the most fundamental. At the lower end, it started with the learning of specifics and moved higher and higher to emphases on comprehension, application, analysis, and synthesis, finally reaching the judgment of knowledge, which was termed, evaluation.

Not long after, Jacob Getzels and Philip Jackson (1962) separated the mental activities that were used to measure intelligence from those that are needed for creativity. The conflation of the two had confused the understanding of children's strengths, and with their research the meaning of learning expanded by another order of magnitude. The idea of curriculum was taking on dimensions that were until then rarely considered. In the same year at Harvard, it needs to be mentioned that Jerome Bruner (1962) added to the breadth of this new thinking by intertwining the value of intrinsic motivation with the role of learning by discovery. Coupled with the discussion was his concern for "inadvertently controlling behavior by imposing irreversible limits upon it with many of our practices in education" (p. 143). The challenge to Skinner, whose office was down the hall, seemed to be complete. Altogether, the whole notion of educational goals now required an even bigger map than the Bloom taxonomy.

Two other of Jerry's teachers had made their marks a few years earlier, but because of this, as professors in the Department of Education, their contributions were bolstered in importance by already standing reputations. Robert Havighurst, with two colleagues in other fields (Warner, Havighurst, and Loeb, 1944) raised a question in the title of their book that would stay around for years to come: *Who Shall Be Educated?* It reverberates in new forms yet today. The title plus the subtitle, *The Challenge of Unequal Opportunities*, stimulated research and discussion that foreshadowed concerns of great magnitude. It was only a ripple at the time, the future significance unanticipated, but it stands as a testimony to the progressive thinking that was a part of this exciting learning environment.

The other professor was Bruno Bettelheim. In 1950, he published *Love Is Not Enough*, a brilliant discussion of the emotional lives of children, based on his work as director of a residential school on campus for a small group of young patients who were profoundly disturbed. Though after his death, he was discredited by many, what was clear then was that the principles he proposed were not critically different for the guidance of normal children. His was a dynamic view of human beings, not one that could be simplified with behavioristic concepts. This view called for an appreciation of the significance of the emotional support that must be integral to the creation of a student's learning environment. The details of how this can be accomplished may not be as he proposed, but the obvious general power of his thinking is in no way lessened, nor does it need to be increased. Providing the emotional support necessary to enhance the process of learning is a serious matter for students of all ages. Education fails to the degree that it is absent. The quality of the learning environment matters, on many levels. This lesson was learned then from his teachings, and it is of the same importance now.

The last star was not as bright, but only because the work of Herbert Thelen (1954) received less recognition than the others. So far ahead of the times, the full breadth of his research on group dynamics is yet to be embraced in educational practice. True enough, attention to small group work and cooperative learning activities have been a part of classroom teaching for many years, but the idea of sustaining a democratic community has never reached the level of concern there is for intellectual and creative learning, nor even the concern for children's emotional lives, no matter how poorly it is managed. What distinguished Thelen was how he, with the help of his graduate students, carried out research in a classroom—one specially designed by him in a way that would facilitate both scholarly investigation and classroom learning. This was totally unusual in those days.

Thelen's conclusions about the classroom environment are obvious on some levels and simultaneously startling when we admit how little has been done to address classroom group dynamics. What he says is a giant challenge for schools even today: "We consider that the school as a small community is maintained and improved through the more or less conscious effort of each citizen to become more effective in his own role; and that this striving, on the part of students, is consonant with the need of youth to de-velop a 'place' for itself in the productive functioning of the com-munity" (Thelen, 1960, p. 160). The rhetoric would not be so star-tling today, but its practice is essentially out of reach. Reading the passage originally was breathtaking—so compelling, but calling for an implausible utopia. His work was regarded beyond the pale, even in this academically adventurous milieu.

Looking back, the University of Chicago days were not attached to the name, *humanistic*. At times, it was associated with *progres-sivism*, but the theories for the most part were thought to be what any mainstream educator ought to be thinking about and apply-ing where possible. Furthermore, though most of the writing achieved national and some international acclaim, it certainly wasn't part of any great wave of reform. It was enough that they gave educators grand ideas to mull on, to consider how schools and classrooms could be different. It's as if it were understood that taking on the full body of research would overwhelm those who were responsible for carrying out the everyday practice of teaching. It was all too different to be taken on as an expected way of ap-proaching teaching and learning.

What we can see in retrospect is how many years it has taken to bring this kind of thinking into the arena of normal problems to solve. From this standpoint, there is a sense of progress in spite of the current array of "intractable" obstacles. For us, what Jerry came away with has been the substance of our theoretical work to-gether, which soon was to begin. In terms of our need to succeed, the measure of how well we were doing was going to be redefined. We had some building bricks out of which to construct a renewed structure of humanistic education.

BEGINNING TO TEACH

Donna's view of education had a very different source. At the time we met, we were drawn to each other because we quickly knew we were living on the same planet. But though we had much in com-mon, there were significant differences. As thoroughly as Jerry's thinking was theoretical, it was her intuition that Donna trusted. To show the degree to which the influence of the research at Chicago didn't travel, Donna's teacher education was abysmal and irrelevant to her. Growing up, she studied acting, taught Sunday school, and was encouraged to be creative by her family. This to-gether with her strong desire to teach differently than she was taught, plus confidence in her intuition, were the tools she had to take on the job of becoming a good teacher in her own eyes. As strongly as Jerry trusted theory, she believed in being practical.

The following letter overlaps two periods of Donna's life, before and after we met. Our dialogue began eight months after she started teaching, and at the time we met, Jerry had only just undertaken his graduate work. What theory he had so far was mostly influenced by Schwab from his undergraduate days. From the beginning, though, it was theory and practice that confronted each other; we both had a new language to learn. Reading the letter from Donna, it should become clearer why this is so:

Dear Dylan,

After thinking a lot about my own schooling, I made every attempt to make my teaching respond to what was missing for me. I needed to find out if it was possible to make education responsive to children's needs while it was also responsive and respectful of the needs of the parents, the community, and the laws of the state. Teachers were required to teach so many minutes per day for each major area of learning. I remember that we had to have 37 minutes of arithmetic each day . . . I may be misremembering that number but it was some silly amount. It was hard to balance all the needs of all the folks who had a stake in public education and add to that the needs of the folks who were supposed to be the primary concern, the students.

I believed that even while learning the required subject matter the children should have a say in how that was happening. I remember trying to make the teaching of phonics interesting and connected to the children who had difficulty. I bought the big fat colored chalk, which the children could use to write on the board. I might say, "Circle the consonant blend in pretty." *The child chose a color and did that. What I remember about that activity is that if I didn't plan to do phonics one morning, I would get complaints from all the children. They loved choosing the color they wanted to use. Such a very simple thing, but it showed me how important simple things are for each of us. I would have loved to have been able to choose a piece of colored chalk to write on the board.*

I was really blessed in 1957 in Wheeling, Illinois, to have had a wonderful principal who supported the way I taught. She visited my classroom often and smiled a lot at what was going on. But, the room was way messier than the other rooms in the school. There were reading centers, paints set up for use when the students were finished with seat work, a snake in an aquarium that the children could take out and handle, paper on the wall for making a mural. The room was messy and lively and my principal really liked it, but there was a problem. When people passed my classroom and looked in, they saw a messy space. She was worried that these adults would be critical of me and how I was teaching. So, she asked me to keep the part of the room that could be seen from the window in the door very neat. She believed that if people came into my room, they would be as pleased as she was with the learning that was going on there.

In third grade at the time, teachers were supposed to teach the children about the different kinds of simple machines. We had a textbook that told about these machines and had pictures of them. I remembered that learning about them was not very interesting to me when I was in third grade, so I thought about what would have been interesting to me. This is what I did. I talked with the class about the six different kinds of simple machines: the lever, inclined plane, wheel and axle, pulley, screw, and wedge. Then I asked each student to write on a piece of paper their first and second choice of machine to study. I was lucky that all the machines were chosen by at least two children! They were then put into groups to figure out how they would teach the whole class about their specific machine. I did give them certain requirements. They had to have a written presentation, a visual one, and a hands-on demonstration of their machine. Each child had to contribute something to each part of the project. Well, Dylan, that was a noisy, lively class for the time we studied machines . . . and we even invited in the second graders to see our projects. I felt good about teaching in this way. I needed to know that each child mattered and was honored.

When children in my class had trouble with learning something and I was busy helping another child, I encouraged them to ask a friend for help. We talked about what it means to help someone and how we should do that. They were not to give the person the answer to the problem or question, but to help them figure out what was stopping them from figuring it out. Of course this did not always run smoothly and it was noisy sometimes, but for the most part the children knew just what to do for their friends and no one had to feel stopped in doing their work.

Not all my principals liked how I taught. In my second year at a new district, the principal and superintendent came to talk to me in December. They pointed out that the children in my classroom were out of their seats more than in any other classroom in the school. They went to the bathroom by themselves and they talked during classes. They said that Mrs. Myers who had taught in my third grade classroom for 42 years never left her desk seat and neither did the children. Why couldn't I be like Mrs. Myers? For some reason I did not get defensive. I simply said that I truly believed that how I was teaching was what children needed and if they did not agree, then they should fire me and get another teacher for my class. Oddly enough, they both got very apologetic and said, "No, no, we want you to teach this class." Neither one ever stepped foot in my classroom after that, and I taught there for two more years.

I did have to struggle to think about every child's needs and of course I was not always successful. One very poignant memory is of Peggy who did not like me one bit, and I am ashamed to say I did not like her either. Not only did I not meet her needs, I was blaming her when she would not participate in the "wonderful" learning experiences I devised. I was sure she was a bad girl. By November, I realized that I was treating Peggy just like my teachers treated me and other children who didn't do what we wanted. I resolved to change how I thought about Peggy. I was her teacher, and I knew I was responsible for making her education work for her. It's a longer story of the change, but the good part is that Peggy and I really came to love each other by the end of the year. Peggy's mother and father came to me then to thank me for making third grade such a fine experience for their daughter. She had always hated school and now she loved coming. I still have the stapler that Peggy gave me as a present at the end of the year.

I am clear that the reason I taught the way I did was to take care of my need to change the education I had as a child. By thinking of my students' needs, I was taking care of my own. Of course, when I helped to create Project Learn School, I was trying to make a place for your mom and your aunt Simone and a place I would love every day. And guess what? I did love it every day as a teacher and mother.

Love, Nana

The language of the letter is in high contrast to the discussion of Jerry's education at the University of Chicago. It illustrates well the difference in languages with which the two of us approached the art and science of teaching. Were we to trace the early development of our teaching skills, the theoretical language could be easily employed to write a reasonable explanation for Jerry—and probably, for Donna as well. But the story that Donna tells, with the contrast between theory and practice it provides, is better served by exploring how our relationship affected the ability to teach. What is clear, at the outset, is that we had a great deal to learn from each other, and this has not changed over the years.

It was refreshing that for the most part our conversations did not engender defensiveness. We recognized that our different skills would be helpful to each other. Today, there are complex notions of reflective teaching and teacher collaboration that have been worked out with careful scholarship to conceptualize our relationship; we had no inkling. The modus operandi (Jerry's words) was to talk (Donna's word). By the time we married, after eight months, we had developed the habit of sharing daily teaching experiences over dinner. Often, the attention was on failures. Some of the time, success took center stage. But mainly, we just told our stories; hearing ourselves aloud heightened our understanding of each other. In later years, the talk sometimes turned into projects where we would team-teach or engage in research together. In the beginning, we were simply overjoyed to find good company for sharing the experience of being beginning teachers.

We were vaguely aware of feeling isolated in our work. This perception was muted by the reality that we weren't working alone. There were other teachers to talk with, friends, and established academics occasionally. Our views, though, were not close enough to theirs. At best, conversations with others had a limited ability to dispel our feelings of isolation; at worst, we would end up aggravating them. The special qualities of our personal relationship tended toward listening, fundamentally more supportive than challenging— but of note, in no way was our support unconditional. In today's terms, we were less critical friends than we were enlightened witnesses for each other. Talking about work transformed our self-awareness, which encouraged reflections about experience from a different angle. The new angle revealed what otherwise would not have been seen.

Practically speaking, the conversations felt good, because they helped us think more clearly, sometimes leading to the solution of a problem, while almost always replacing the feelings of isolation with companionship and confidence. We each knew that someone authentic thought well of our efforts. We were surrounded by support, but not without challenge. And for the most part, there was the supposition that the responsibility for challenge fell on oneself. In time, we would understand how this responsibility was no less than what we hoped for students to develop.

COLLABORATIVE CONVERSATION

Theoretically, attention should be given, not to the locus of the responsibility for challenge, but to the need to talk and actively be heard. We had uncovered a teacher's need hidden below the surface. Here was a desire that in the process of being met addressed all other needs. Whether or not a person wants to be in charge of challenge, the daily pressures need attention. There is no such thing as solving all of the problems that constantly face us, but they require management, if only to do a bit of triage, set priorities, or set a few aside for now without repression, which only causes them to fester. Not every need it turns out is attached to a sense of serious disappointment. Without someone with whom to share one's thoughts, the lack of full awareness may not be noticeable. But what is evident, when it is brought to the surface, is the need to talk. Judging from what happens when the energy is released, talking about oneself is like blood pumping, breathing, and eating. Everyone has a story to tell, and there is good reason not to wait for a special occasion.

The collaborative conversation in mind, however, does have special conditions to assure its quality. In our case, there was a blending of theory and practice, which explained the impact we had on each other. Beyond the failures, successes, and plain talk, there would grow a collaboration that went far beyond the words that were shared. But from experience, we now know that much of the benefit of the relationship depends on how it facilitates small shifts in thinking and subsequent actions. The content is not limited to discussions of theory and practice; it is determined by differences in personalities that enter into the interaction. The result is a friendship dedicated to an ongoing collaborative conversation. Sometimes, the process has the potential to turn ordinary snapshots of teaching experiences into Ansel Adams photographs of wondrous landscapes that inspire the dialogue with meaning. Something less can still make the effort worthwhile, even when the scene portrayed is upsetting.

But equally true, finding partners to work with is work itself. In lots of ways, it is not preferred for life partners to have both kinds of relationship. The good feelings we have for working with each other have grown over nearly fifty years, sustained by the stamina required to have enough fun to survive the hard parts of growing and staying connected. We too depend on other teachers and researchers for collaborations or partnerships for the time we are engaged in one job, project, or another. One of the first conditions for this kind of relationship is a mutual feeling of equality. Our teachers, mentors, superiors, students, and even busybodies all have had a formative part in our development as a whole, but a good friend who is a bit like ourselves, deserved by everyone, is a special gift. For teaching, for sure, we're not talking about a life-long partner as the optimal avenue. A fellow teacher is great, but just as well, a small compatible group can be formed for the purpose of talking about teaching. Furthermore, people come and go in our lives; it's not a bad idea to be on the lookout for new people who might be interested. Teaching alone isn't the end of the world; it's just that the need for collaborative conversation will be unmet. And, sometimes, there can be too much talking while not getting enough done. As always, we have never found panaceas, just hopeful possibilities.

Good listening is of great importance, and it's a two-way requirement. Partly, this means the patience to listen at length. But it also includes keeping the focus, while responding, on the concerns of the person who is doing the talking, without changing the focus to another topic or onto oneself until the time feels right, unlike chatting in a more social setting. For any quality conversation, there is no script or a tight set of rules with which to adhere. Even interruptions are a lively part of stimulating discussions. Still, in good faith, one should be able to trust that stories will be given enough time to feel substantially heard. There is room for sharing a similar story, a bit of advice, lots of empathy, and even more words that convey an interested and curious understanding. But too much advice, too many questions, or tangents detract from the feeling that the need to talk is being met. All this is turned around when it's someone else's turn to be the focus of the conversation.

One of the toughest conditions is to tell the truth, because it is not easy to do this while avoiding excessive criticism. There has to be a place for challenge, but tempering it is essential. As teachers in the classroom, we at times forget that criticism, or even a challenge hampered with implied disappointment, can be too difficult to incorporate without a sufficiently supportive context. In talking and listening among equals, the problem affects the feelings of being heard. Yet, saying something we don't believe is to undermine a friendship of any kind. The dilemma crosses through relationships regularly, and here a particular problem is how it interferes with the clarity needed to improve teaching skills.

There is no right answer to the conflicting pressures to be truthful and, at the same time, supportive. The practical answer depends primarily on a creative blending of sympathy and a close look at the many-sided dimensions that contribute to experience. Stories usually have a group of players connected with the drama, some on stage, some off. Generally, the listener has the advantage of not being as embroiled in the reality as the teller of the story. There's a better chance of avoiding prejudice, stereotypes, and stymied thinking. Listeners, too, have less at stake in making a mistake in how they listen. There's really no good purpose to fear mistakes, on anybody's part; they are going to happen. There is even the possibility that an episode of poor listening, honestly admitted, can lead to a good laugh, and humor is an equally good road for changing the angle of the view.

The remaining conditions are similar to guidelines for maintaining close relationships in general. Caring about each other's feelings is necessary as is a willingness to learn from mistakes and being open to change. Maybe they could go without mentioning, yet noting them emphasizes the purpose of collaborative conversation. More than ordinary talking, and different from a contract with a teacher or some similar role where challenge is invited, the aim in this relationship is to clarify how goals conceived and set by oneself can be achieved. The partner's role is to support the possibility of realizing these personal ideals, even when they seem a bit out of reach. Ideals are well served from knowing that there is someone else who cares about them—who trusts at some level that practical applications will be found. For the teacher who is talking, it is an especially helpful moment, because it is free of mistakes. Sometimes, no judge can be harder on mistakes than oneself. The openness to change includes a willingness to alter one's self-concept. Caring for each other, knowing that mistakes are part of the bargain, and anticipating difficult personal changes make a significant agenda. Sharing it with a trusted friend is courageous and smart.

The storyteller has to decide what to do on Monday, to figure out the practical answers. The listener has less responsibility, but still a difficult task of mustering the patience and stamina to listen well, be honest, be caring, and be open as well to mistakes and change. The tricky work is finding honest responses without undermining trust in the ability of others to meet their own challenges. But, when the listener decides to bring up a challenge or a criticism, it should consider whether this is the right time and place for feedback. It certainly shouldn't happen too often. The main purpose of the conversation is to maintain the spirit to stay with our ideals and on the job. More than this is possible, but not necessary. The strategy we have worked out over the years stresses the importance of small shifts that make a difference.

We have to beware of the seesaw. At the top, there is the exuberance that comes with being a teacher. At the bottom, there is a mud puddle of despair. We have so much to offer. But as much, there lurks a sense of failure that can undo us. We are supposed to be heroes, but too often the teacher is the culprit. The support we give to one another keeps us out of the mud puddles.

5

The Psychology of Teaching and Learning

Donna's letter to Dylan that follows is about Jerry's work at Temple University. His tenure spanning from 1968 until retirement in 1998 included chairing the Department of Psychoeducational Processes, regularly teaching undergraduates and graduate students the Art and Science of Teaching, and doing research on humanistic practices in elementary, high school, and college classrooms. Donna urged him, even insisting on occasion, to model the theoretical aspects of the research by bringing them to life in his college classrooms—and to take time periodically to teach children in their classrooms.

Dear Dylan,

Now that you are old enough to read this letter, it won't come as a surprise for me to say that your Grangran Jerry was an unusually fine teacher. His teaching primarily took place at Temple University, but every now and then he came to Project Learn to assist teachers in their classrooms. All of the PL teachers with whom he taught loved having him work with them and their children. Not only was he loving and respectful, he was funny and creative. He was always thinking of new ways to teach something for a particular child. Some of his ideas were pretty wild and we would laugh at them, but most made us reconsider how to serve the students in the best way possible.

Jerry taught courses at the university to young people who intended to become teachers. Unlike the professors of education that I endured in my college education, he was lively and interesting. He taught his courses in the way that he hoped his students would teach their students some day. He didn't just tell them what they should do; he lived what he believed worked best for educating people of all different kinds of abilities and interests.

By the time we came to Philadelphia in 1968, there were many books written about alternative ways of educating. Both of us felt very supported by these texts for we had been doing much of what was suggested and now we had a community of educators talking and writing about this shift in education. Most of what was written was about young children not about adult students. Jerry was using these ideas with adults. I really do know how he taught, because I took a few of his courses and taught with him at times.

I have a humorous memory of being in his class for the first time. He first described five different ways to work on the particular subject we were studying. He asked us to divide ourselves into groups of about four to six students and choose one of the five different ways. I joined a group, and we began to do the task he had asked us to do. While we were waiting for the other groups to finish their work, some of the women in the group started talking about Jerry. Fortunately all of what they said was positive but some was a bit embarrassing. You see, I hadn't told anyone my last name, and they did not know I was the professor's wife. Well, someone said he was a very handsome man and wondered if he was married. Before anyone could say anything more, I went to him and whispered that he had to introduce me or things could get quite uncomfortable. He smiled, put his arm around me and interrupted the class to tell them we were married, and when I returned to my group, there were several people blushing. I assured them that I was in no way offended, only pleased that they thought highly of my husband and friend.

He provided opportunities for students to have small teaching experiences before they worked with a large group of students. He formed groups in his class that were designed for the students to teach a concept to the whole class. But before they did, they taught their own group, which was only six or seven people. Then, they were given assignments to teach one child some concept and to report on that experience to the class. They had at least a bit of practice when they went out to a school to work for three hours a week with a teacher. Now it is not unusual for pre-service teachers to have several small teaching assignments before beginning their student teaching. Then it was very unusual.

Not only did I take courses with Jerry, many of the other PL teachers did as well. We asked all student teachers who came from other universities to take his course so that they would understand experientially what it means to learn in a humanistic educational environment. Almost none of us experienced this kind of learning as we grew up. Having an education that is responsive to our needs was an idea, not a reality. Taking Jerry's class made the idea real for many PL teachers and student teachers.

Throughout our years as educators the two of us talked extensively about what we were doing and what changes needed to be made to continue our growth as teachers. One important memory is of Jerry coming home one evening very frustrated. He talked a great deal about the students in his course that he called "jocks." They were this and they were that and they were not doing what they should be doing. It was football season, these young men were playing hard games of football every weekend, and it seemed they were not very attentive to the work in class. I challenged Jerry by asking if he would ever group any other students together and give them a name. Of course not. And immediately, he realized that he was exhibiting a prejudice toward these athletes. He had grouped them and no longer thought about them as individuals. So, we sat a long time and talked about each student individually and just what seemed to be happening for that person. By the time he went to his next class, he no longer had "jocks" in his class; he had several young men who needed different kinds of support and challenges from him. What touches me most about this experience is the ability of your Grangran to see his mistake and to change without getting defensive.

Talking about teaching with Jerry was and is such a rich experience. I wish that every teacher could have conversations like these with a colleague.

Love, Nana

TEACHING AND LEARNING TOGETHER

The story at the end of the letter is a good example of what we mean by collaborative conversation. Clearly, Jerry wasn't meeting the needs of his students in the best way possible, not even close. The example illustrates how an openness to challenge functions in a productive way. Furthermore, the dialogue models what we expect of students, even when they are not there to witness the interchange. Modeling learning, of course, is important in the face-to-face activity of the classroom, but the effects are equally valuable when evidenced in a teacher's change of attitude that is likely to come about with the insights. Dialogue such as this ideally belongs in teacher education workshops and courses in continuing education, which are helpful in many ways. But they are not as likely to connect with daily ongoing classroom problems—what we might better call here continuous learning. No less, the expectation is reasonable for students. That challenge often sets off defensiveness is not surprising. Modeling a willingness to confront problems has the potential for teaching students how to work at keeping themselves open to the challenges that a teacher presents.

LESSONS FROM THE 1960S

Looking back, it was the historical context of the 1960s and the early 1970s that implicitly provided support for the creation by Jerry and his colleagues of a Department of Psychoeducational Processes. Alternative educational programs were sprouting up everywhere, but for the most part were aimed at elementary and high school students. A unique program created by the board of directors of a university, Temple opened the department's doors in the fall of 1970. Amidst a cultural revolution, there was high interest in the study of group dynamics to better understand the role of a facilitator in teaching and training. Along with this interest came the need to know more about humanistic theory for the everyday practice of teaching, particularly children.

The 1960s and early 1970s were marked by a unique cultural upheaval that is remembered mostly for the liberties that college students and the younger generation of adults in general took in response to traditional social norms. However, it was a time as well that confronted civil rights, the war in Vietnam, and social injustice on other fronts. Progressive educational dialogue rode on this wave with an ease that caused many fewer negative ripples than other more pressing concerns. The experimental schools that resulted provided new opportunities for expressing and meeting underlying needs that had been largely ignored. For all the changes that had come about since the turn of the twentieth century, a much-changed view of meaningful education started up again. Over the next fifty years, there was a shift in how children should be taught that has matured into what has become common expectations. These expectations are routinely frustrated by how badly the mark is missed, but the bar for today's standards got its first big boost during this period.

It was a time for rebuilding the foundations of education; these developments reached across the turn of the twenty-first century. For educators, there were widespread opportunities to expand humanistic practices, and many of these effects were long lasting. It was a particularly good time for teachers to experiment with humanistic practices in their classrooms. What surprised and encouraged us during these years were the great strides taken by practitioners, not necessarily theoreticians, to introduce changes in schools that challenged the status quo throughout the United States and abroad. Frequently, administrators were responsible for introducing school-wide programs, and college professors helped out in the creation of new alternative schools, but many more classroom teachers for the first time acted as if they were in charge. The contribution of academic studies followed closely behind, but the changes were mostly initiated by teachers who were dissatisfied with what was then common practice. Other stakeholders stood aside enough to sustain the innovations motivated and applied by the practitioners. The impact on all stakeholders resulted in a grander vision of quality education—which on occasion has actually been attained.

The giants among these stakeholders were the teachers who wrote stories about their efforts and successfully found popular markets for their writing. Their influence was widespread, at the least, across English-speaking countries. The tallest among them, so to speak, was A. S. Neill (1992), the founder of the Summerhill School and author of a book about it, first published in 1960, having sold over 4 million copies since then. And, the book is still in print. He described a small school in England whose roots go back to 1921, where students of all ages go to class only if they choose, participate as voting members at regular school meetings where significant decisions are made about the program, and where teachers who cannot respect students' needs are not hired. Typically, readers of this book react as if it is a school where there is no structure; in fact, it has a complex set of boundaries that serve to maintain a functional educational program. No doubt, it is one that is far removed from what most everyone else has ever experienced. The kind of school it presents is indeed radical and in so many ways impractical in the larger world, nor has it even been a successful model for structuring other schools in any long-lasting way.

Why have so many people read this book? Why have teacher educators assigned it to their students? Some mocked Neill's ideas in order to promote more traditional education. More typically, in our experience, it struck a chord that signaled what was missing for them in their schooling. It stimulated wondering about what schools could be like if one held a grander vision. Educators, and parents too, were very curious, as were others. In high contrast to the practical limitations of Neill's stories about Summerhill, it was its existence in the real world that undermined assumptions about the limitations of children. Certainly, context makes a huge difference, but this raises an intriguing question. What would happen if the context of any teacher were changed in some way, large or small? Ignoring the challenge of creating a school like Summerhill, it is possible to focus on the assumptions carried in a school that is familiar to a teacher. Would the capabilities of these children be affected by practicing a special kind of suspended disbelief? Or better, expanded belief? Might a teacher's actions be altered? Would children's competence be revealed where it hadn't before? The fact that the Summerhill School has kept its doors open to students for over eighty years—now directed by his daughter, Zoë Neill Readhead—together with its effect on many readers, tells a story of its own.

What followed was the writing by other classroom teachers, each reaching significantly large audiences in the United States and elsewhere. There was a substantial popular interest in education in the 1960s. Though the efforts of these teacher-writers were not as successful as *Summerhill* in the long run, a reasonable cause for discouragement, there is another way to look at their achievements with the perspective of time.

For example, what John Holt (1964) wrote about the meaning of learning in *How Children Fail* still stands as insightful. Here was an experienced teacher who after many years in the classroom offered a compelling list of criteria for what he called *real learning*. It starts with being able to state the learning in one's own words, and it is followed by the ability to give examples, recognize it in various guises, see connections between it and other ideas, make use of it, foresee some of its consequences, and state its opposite. He acknowledged that only some of these criteria would be enough to qualify as real learning and admitted that the list wasn't necessarily complete. Yet, this simple list carried a potent definition. He had a handle on a simple truth that is sensible even when present-day relativism is in the forefront. Most teachers would probably not be as articulate, but the overwhelming agreement that the ubiquitous testing undergone by children today for measuring their reading and math abilities is intrusive speaks to a wider understanding about what real learning is. Holt set this truth in motion forty years ahead of his time.

In two more acclaimed books, we saw the raw experience of teachers facing extremely difficult classrooms with an openness to their own vulnerability and a commitment to a creative response to their students' needs. Herbert Kohl (1967) taught thirty-six children in a ghetto school, and Eleanor Craig (1972) a smaller class of emotionally disturbed children, around seven depending on the week. They took on the worries that Holt (1964) expressed in answer to how children fail: "because they are afraid, bored, and confused" (p. xiii). These stumbling blocks were their starting points. Their experiences were so difficult that the numbers either way hardly factored into the overwhelming challenges they faced each day. The stories they told of successes, and even the failures, inspired readers, uplifting their hopes for education in their own settings. Here were compelling stories that taught lessons about the powerful effects of teachers on how competent children can become. The lessons stood in place even when realizing that the energies of these teachers were nearly sapped dry. The impact was not about the long-range success of the teachers or the students. It was about the possible. Altogether, these two teachers and the children they taught were trailblazers. What we learned about is what it takes to make a difference—in spite of our limitations. The story in the end is everyone's: what can "I" do that works for me and for my students when the power of assumptions is altered, even if only slightly?

The efforts of teachers like Neill, Holt, Kohl, and Craig also had effects on other teachers who were founding small schools that had humanistic teaching in mind. But many of the new alternative schools were aimed at meeting the needs of middle- and upper-class children. Using these contemporary influences as well as bringing into focus the work of Dewey from a generation before, George Dennison (1969) told the story of the First Street School in New York City for poor children. Necessarily, financial support was obtained from outside the community. For children whose parents did not have the resources to set up an innovative program on their own, Dennison as a part-time teacher in partnership with three full-time teachers, plus other part-timers who provided additional kinds of expertise, formed a small utopia. They were able to pay attention to each individual student, all the while building a community of students and teachers that welcomed the participation of the students' parents.

The classes were small. With only twenty-three students enrolled, the opportunities for each child to succeed were considerable. There were degrees of choice that made the program look dramatically unlike typical schools for students who were not privileged. There was room for the idiosyncratic quirks of students, and teachers, and the strong possibility of successfully developing lessons that built on children's individual needs and strengths. Along the same lines, there was room for teachers to insist on the adherence to a few fundamental norms that kept the community functioning—no hitting, no bullying, and no destroying classroom materials. Resolving other conflicts of interest often could be done where no one felt they were losing respect. The emphasis was on working out disagreements one on one, so that the most figural concerns could be kept on teaching and learning.

Is it criticism or approval to judge this endeavor a utopia? Once again, the model is not a candidate for widespread adaptation in public or private schools elsewhere. As a criticism, the accomplishments of the First Street School can fairly be ignored. On the other hand, we saw the efforts of these teachers as a model toward which to strive. Dennison reported, "We treated the children with consideration and justice. I don't mean that we never got angry and never yelled at them (nor they at us). I mean that we took seriously the pride of life that belongs to the young—even to the very young. We did not coerce them in violation of their proper independence. Parents and children both found that they very much approved of this" (Dennison, 1969, p. 8). The attitude conveyed could be expressed by any teacher and is deserved by every student. How it plays out in different situations would be unique, but as a foundation for teacher-student interaction, it is doable on some level.

It might be argued that only in a tiny school like this was it possible for such an attitude to be regularly expressed, mainly because the resources seem to measure up greater than those provided by even a wealthy school district. To insist, though, that substantially caring for students' needs is wholly impractical is just not so. The practicality of a cooperative community project offsets a sense of an unattainable utopia. The staff at the school exhibited an attitude that supports cooperation; the school was an environment where mutually supportive relationships developed. But, after two years, the money ran out and the school closed. It's a shame.

Meanwhile, another idealistic program had been developing in England, but in no way a utopia. Joseph Featherstone (1971), an American reporter, brought news of reforms that had had widespread support. What was called informal education had been introduced in many infant and junior schools, for children ages five to eleven or twelve. Unlike the Summerhill School and the other examples discussed so far, the program was countrywide. And, it was noteworthy that the emphasis was specifically on reforming the curriculum where classrooms at Summerhill looked much like those anywhere else. Early on, the prevalent focus was on the teacher-student relationship. Reforms stimulated by the informal education program in England had much more to do with how the curriculum should be taught. Students rarely met as a whole. Classrooms were set up with multiple-learning centers, and students usually worked in small groups or alone. Choices about what to learn each day, the most idealistic element of informal education, were usually left up to the students. The reforms in England substantially influenced what became known in the United States as the open classroom.

To be sure, the concept of informal education was not accepted in most schools in England, but it was a major contender for reform everywhere in the country. What stunned us was how the reforms affected large elements of primary education. Though the figures are unclear, as many as a third of the infant schools might have been involved, and though many fewer, the number of junior schools that took on aspects of the reforms was counted as significant. The attitude of the teachers was similar to those in the other innovative schools we knew about, but clearly as a whole what was happening took place on a grander scale. And though it wasn't primarily the teachers who initiated these changes, their enthusiasm was a major factor in the successes they achieved. Featherstone told a story that was compelling to a large audience that included educators and anyone else interested in education.

No school program lasts forever, and so it is in England today that the larger reforms achieved during the 1960s are no longer in the limelight. Surely, the lack of resources that are now provided for education, there as in the United States, has undone many of them. But the achievements added in a unique way to the larger picture we are describing—differently than the ongoing success of Summerhill, which we mainly judged by its persistence. Added to Summerhill's challenge of the assumptions made about the capabilities of children, a fundamental contribution, are these newer reforms that tackled an equally difficult problem. It was the creation of new methods of teaching to match a different set of assumptions about how children best learn. The concept of informal education provided a model for loosening lock-step teaching in the classroom. Together, they offered a more complete model for educators to meet the needs of the teacher and the students in schools that have their own unique mold. The idea of almost never holding a whole-class meeting is not likely to work for most teachers today, but providing meaningful choices to all children is essential to making a learning environment more humanistic.

The whole of English primary education was in no way radically transformed; many, maybe most, of the faults of years of tradition were left unattended. But the changes were widespread and seen in many schools all over the country. What did get fixed supports the argument that humanistic changes are doable in settings too readily assumed to be unaccepting and impenetrable. Not only do humanistic changes allow for a broader spectrum of educational goals, changes like these improve the chance that the goals set by a teacher will more readily be accomplished. What occurred opened a path to make room for teachers to better meet students' needs. Featherstone's report evidenced that even in classes with as many as forty students, the methods of informal education are not impossible. The work, he concluded, is harder for teachers, the classrooms are noisier, but he was impressed by how diligently the students worked. The reforms stand as a useful model to be adapted for any classroom, any classroom that is, where a teacher wants to better meet the needs of every student.

In New Zealand, a wonderful teacher had confronted the problems she was facing with a classroom of Maori children (Ashton-Warner, 1963). It's unclear what educational theories and practices had reached down under to influence Sylvia Aston-Warner, but there is no doubt that her teaching foreshadowed and was in tune with the not-so-turbulent cultural revolution by the time it reached the Northern Hemisphere. Her book *Teacher* was a great success. "The year's best book on education," said *Time Magazine*. Using insights and intuitions that her teaching experiences had engendered, her influence on the educational climate of the times proved the power of the efforts of one lone creative teacher.

Maori children had proved to be difficult students in schools based on traditions that had come from England when New Zealand was colonized. Overall, Maori children were strangers inside buildings that housed the Western classroom, and the curriculum was even stranger. The notion of multiple learning centers would have been an anathema to the students; certainly "centers" weren't part of her thinking. Choice was high on her list, but the ordinary choices the students made each day had nothing to with what they wanted to study, in the sense of which subject. The choices were about the words that meant something to them, words that have intense meaning. She encouraged conversation about the difficulties of their lives that were different and more severe than for other children in New Zealand. With words from these conversations, Ashton-Warner built materials for lessons in reading and writing. She built the curriculum on what she called key vocabularies, private key vocabularies, organic reading, and organic writing. She recognized the significance of creating a context that welcomed students into the teaching and learning environment: "The method of teaching any subject in a Maori infant room may be seen as a plank in a bridge from one culture to another" (Ashton-Warner, 1963, p. 28).

* * *

The lessons from the 1960s are not prescriptions; they are ideas that can be fitted to a particular context within which a teacher is teaching. Most of all, they are practical, because they have stood the test of application. The degree to which they were successful along the lines of criteria that measure this success is less important than the fact that they worked for the teacher who applied them. Yet, they are useful as evidence if a teacher sees them this way, and even then, it's not only about the size of the sample. Large programs, small programs, or one teacher doing her or his job are all in a position to provide ideas about how to better meet students' needs—to prove that a way of teaching is possible, somewhere.

It is easy to assume (again) that children's learning is hampered when they are provided a range of opportunities that give them a large degree of choice. It is too easy to say that children aren't ready for this kind of responsibility. More realistically, we can understand how children need different kinds of structure to enhance the effectiveness of their learning environment. Some of these differences can exist in the same classroom, some in the same school, and some not. What might not conflict with school policies? How might today's students respond? And, their parents? What are my strengths as a teacher? What can I get away with and still believe that I won't lose my job?

HUMANISTIC THEORY

Theoretical writing about humanistic teaching helped educators in the late 1960s and on to articulate why innovative programs were important and how they can function successfully. It wasn't enough to give children more freedom in the classroom. It wasn't helpful to confront students more than once in a while with the question, "What do you want to do today?" A workable learning environment that strives to build mutually supportive relationships and to provide a wide range of choices requires attention to the dynamic needs of everyone who is involved. There are concerns that relate to how the curriculum is organized and presented to students. All teachers, including humanistic ones, are responsible for letting their students know what they are expected to learn. It is not always easy to figure out how to do this when the other side of the balance is leaving room for meaningful choices. And, teaching that is built on providing an array of choices often has to confront students who resist the responsibility it carries. The notion of learning by discovery, for example, is laden with obstacles. Habits developed in earlier learning limit risk-taking both on the part of the students and the teacher.

There is a special tension in a humanistic classroom that is less likely to occur in other classrooms. In addition to letting students know what is expected of them in connection with the curriculum, there is also the task of providing guidance for taking on major responsibility for one's own learning. The problem of successfully managing this tension resides in understanding what intrigues students. It is not just the subject matter and the intrinsic excitement that can accompany learning about the subject; it is also how choice is structured that can tap a parallel excitement. Whereas the first has to do mostly with the adventure of knowing, offering students meaningful choice is knowing that mutually supportive relationships in the classroom are essential—discovering that learning is essentially a cooperative enterprise.

In a yearlong study of the infant school classrooms, Lillian Weber (1971) struggled with the definition of informal education. She was an American visiting England to investigate how the infant school functioned with the intention of bringing home insights about the basic concepts that might be helpful. In her mind, what she saw clearly demonstrated that the children were experiencing a high-quality education. However, it was unaccompanied by a needed definition, and this she worked out on her own. At first, it seemed that the concept of activity methods would suffice, but as time passed she changed her mind. In conclusion, informal education "came to have a broader meaning for me than the description of methods. . . . Informal, as I understand it, refers to the setting, the arrangements, the teacher-child and child-child relationships that maintain, restimulate if necessary, and extend what is considered to be the most intense form of learning, the already existing child's way of learning through play and through the experiences he *(sic)* seeks out for himself" (pp. 10–11).

An intriguing contrast to Weber's travels in England was Joseph Schwab's thinking at the University of Chicago amidst the turmoil of the student protests during the 1960s. Schwab, as an educator who had never much paid attention to nursery or elementary school teaching, a college professor *sine qua non,* would not have been expected to liken a student's inquiry to play, but certainly, his thinking attached the idea of learning to experiences that students seek out for themselves. In 1969, he published *College Curriculum and Student Protest,* and writes, "The curriculum can put such materials, facilities, occasions, and invitations in the way of the student that he is moved and enabled to pursue enquiries [Schwab's spelling] in his own right: focus on an interest of his own, shape a problem concerning it, search out materials, choose his methods, apply them, formulate the products of his enquiry" (pp. 89–90).

Years later, Lee Shulman (1991) reflecting on Schwab's career said the book was an outcome of "his shock at the character of student demonstrations at Chicago against the war in Vietnam. It was not the political beliefs of the protesters that upset him; he may well have agreed with their political inclinations. He was taken aback by the unwillingness of the student leaders, many of them outstanding students in the College, to permit the free flow of ideas" (p. 456). From very different starting points, Schwab and Weber provided a way of thinking about learning that is much the same. Students are expected to learn through discovery, and from this vantage, there is an ongoing world of choice. Though, neither of them would have had the concept of mutually supportive relationships on their minds, Weber's concerns related to interpersonal relationships in elementary school classrooms were close to the idea. And, it is no surprise that Schwab, as a philosopher, in his frustration with the protesting college students was onto fundamental problems underlying the dynamics of interpersonal conflict, at the least unconsciously.

Shulman and Evan Keislar (1966) with the contributions of ten of their colleagues reviewed the range of thinking that was the topic of a special conference set up to evaluate learning by discovery. The conference was aimed at achieving a better understanding of the differences between telling students answers as an effective way of teaching versus pushing them to figure out the answers for themselves. Problematically, many of the concerns were related to the best ways to acquire specific knowledge that a teacher is already certain to know. Characteristic of the time, the motivation for the conference was to settle questions about the advantages and disadvantages of these two strategies, which often amounted to which is better. Even today, we are not out of these woods, but we are more likely to know that this is not the most productive path to follow. And still, what they uncovered clarified that how the study of learning is formulated is a big factor in developing sound advice for teachers. Wisely, it was concluded that in general there is no way to know how much guidance a teacher should give nor could a single teaching method accomplish a full range of teaching objectives. Much depends on the specific context.

It was already known then that to offer choice requires paying attention to the meaning it has for students. Trivial choices will be noticed and can lead to not paying attention to them, benignly or obstructively. Justly so. Jerome Bruner, one of the conference participants, in *Toward a Theory of Instruction* (1966), further developed the importance of intrinsic motivation that he had earlier attached to learning by discovery. Two of his main concepts pointed toward the source of meaningful choice: curiosity and the need for competence. His high regard for the relevance of curiosity was based on how ubiquitously it is observed in the behavior of children early in their development. It is one of the essences of a healthy child. Thus, the productive use of freedom given to students is facilitated by aspects of the curriculum that tap their curiosity. Opportunities for following up on where one's curiosity leads are a sure bet for initiating successful learning.

But, the teacher has to organize elements of the curriculum so that there is a good probability that students can effectively continue the process through to some successful point. Because, Bruner argued, the human learner also has a need for competence—with curiosity, equally a part of intrinsic motivation. It is possible that the experience of following where curiosity leads can end up frustrating students. It is necessary to begin by asking, where does the student's freedom best fit in the learning process? As always, teachers have to make their own set of choices, and in this case they are better named hunches. For knowledge, which has correct answers, it may be enough to choose from a set of learning tasks. The freedom is about determining what feels like a good personal learning strategy. Choice is related to a broad range of learning strategies: for example, whether to study alone, with others in a small group, or in a lecture—all of the above, some of the above, none of the above. Maybe, it could make sense for the student to invent a different, unique strategy.

The possibilities particularly relate to how much there is to be discovered. Some subjects are best taught as a set of relatively sure facts. Other subjects are better taught as a study of information in order to form one's own opinions. Sometimes, learning is about really finding out information that the teacher doesn't know. The universe of learning is itself a big unknown. Choices related to reading and math skills have more to do with how the student learns best. For social sciences, there is plenty of room for students to make up their own minds. In the arts, setting up even more open-ended inquiries is often easy. The teaching of science is a collage of different worlds, and the world of choices itself expands just as we expand our notions of how knowledge can otherwise be expanded.

So it was in the 1960s that what students should be learning was itself expanded to what was called the affective domain. Adding to the classification of educational goals that appeared in what became the first volume of *The Taxonomy of Educational Objectives*, edited by Benjamin Bloom (1956), he with two collaborators edited a second *Taxonomy* (Krathwohl, Bloom, and Masia, 1964). Their objectives introduced concern for learning that heightened awareness, responsiveness, commitment, the ability to conceptualize values, and an interest in creating a personal worldview. What was missing for us was greater attention to the learning needed to understand how to live more comfortably with others. There wasn't a direct focus on the immense importance of interpersonal relationships in human learning. Learning is essentially a cooperative enterprise; human life is all about connectedness between people. Now years later, from observing and working with children, we have come to see how learning is so much about building mutually supportive relationships. Intuitively, they seem to know as much about this as we do. Not only does it affect how they get along with others, it is an important part of their cognitive learning as well.

We saw more clearly how the planning of teaching is only partly intertwined with the subject matter. The other critical part has to do with the relationship between the teacher and the students, and students with their peers. Rooted in a discussion of human needs, Abraham Maslow (1962, 1968) deepened an understanding of how choice enters into the dynamics of learning and our relationships with others. Choice is often about how much students can handle, as an individual and as a member of a group of varying sizes. With an awareness of the need for competence (Bruner, 1966), there is an interplay between the need for a safe, supportive learning environment and the delight that comes from being challenged. But, the need for adequate safety is stronger than the need for growth that challenge offers to satisfy. How does one make this choice? Maslow (1968) argues, "if free choice is *really* free and if the chooser is not too sick or frightened to choose, he will choose wisely, in a healthy and growthful direction, more often than not" (p. 48). Because of individual differences, what varies is the willingness and ability to take responsibility. Add to the mix the obvious: teachers' time and energies are not unlimited. There is always a kind of triage going on in the classroom. Students, and teachers too, need to feel safe enough to manage challenge.

It was Rogers (1969) in *Freedom to Learn* who provided the most comprehensive discussion of how to teach creatively and effectively within the dynamics of a humanistic classroom. From the broadest perspective, the goal is to build trusting relationships in all directions. With trust comes the sense of safety and the willingness to accept challenge. The role of the teacher's guidance then is to modify the difficulties that challenges present in ways that, in her or his estimation, will likely allow students to succeed. Without guarantees, he argued that what is required from teachers is realness, acceptance, and empathic understanding. The triage faced now is not the tension between two polar pressures, safety and challenge, but three pressures that are expressed in a dynamic drama that takes place in the classroom, with or without awareness and sensitivity. For realness, teachers have to work hard at achieving their goals while maintaining a sense of authenticity. This means that compromises are made without a loss of integrity. Generally, it also means that the teachers will be able to maintain a sense of agency, and humor. Here, significantly, is the locus of the challenges that a teacher offers—they are meant to express a teacher's vision of what students can learn.

All the while, the teacher must find opportunities to consistently accept students' contributions to their own learning. It won't work to provide phony compliments; it's a matter of pointing to the strengths that reveal themselves in a student's efforts. And though empathy helps the teacher to do this job, this internal emotional work of the mind and heart is more connected with the prior job of setting the level of challenge so that success is likely. Luckily, knowing how to succeed at this task is easier than learning how to win at a casino but sometimes, not by much. Nevertheless, this is how students build a history of competence that can sustain them when they don't succeed. Realness, acceptance, and empathy are the signposts of humanistic teaching, as they have become for talk therapy of all persuasions. The result of their dynamic interactions makes it possible for students to master the curriculum partly as a function of developing mutually supportive relationships, in an interplay where both the intellectual and emotional aspects of teaching and learning help make the other possible.

OPEN TEACHING AND LEARNING

The Department of Psychoeducational Processes at Temple University was founded within the setting of the developing humanistic ideas, concepts, theories, and scholarly investigations. Jerry served as the first chairperson, under the leadership of Dean Paul Eberman, also a graduate of the University of Chicago, with four more graduates from Chicago, nearly half of the entire faculty. The program stood out because it was a practical example of its own philosophy and psychology. Teaching mirrored the theories that students were learning, and faculty, support staff, and students were all invited to participate in making the majority of the decisions involved in the running of the program. The PEP program, as it was called for short, was Summerhill in spirit and in practice to the extent that Dean Eberman could manage within the structure of the university. Sometimes, its reputation alone was enough to raise the hackles of faculty outside the department.

It was also in this setting that Jerry with two colleagues published *The Psychology of Open Teaching and Learning* (Silberman, Allender, and Yanoff, 1972). The book included the writings of many of the practitioners and theoreticians that we've been discussing, plus articles by the authors, and it served as a text for courses in the department and for other students all over the country. As a practical guide for college professors, inquiry activities were included to engage students in theories and methods for the design of stimulating learning environments, to deepen understanding of cognitive and affective learning processes, and to broaden conceptions of the role of a teacher in the classroom. The book wasn't on any bestseller list, but it did create opportunities to discuss humanistic teaching for a wide audience of future educators.

The program was disbanded in 1998, the year Jerry retired. Why? Politics, turf, and a change of the academic climate are all part of understanding what happened. But, it is also reasonable to believe, as Lawrence Cremin argued for the long-range influences of progressive education in the first half of the twentieth century, that the work the faculty set out to do had been accomplished. Over twenty-eight years, many hundreds of graduates went off to teach, train, and lead in professions that stretched from classroom teachers and school administrators to educators in the vastly different fields of business, health care, public service, and even in religious and military service. These people came to the program with concerns for learning how to introduce aspects of humanistic teaching in their chosen fields. By the time the program doors were closed, many of these ideas had become commonplace.

Confronted with difficult demands, these graduates have had opportunities to teach from the position of their strengths, interests, and strategies. A lot has to do with beliefs that are supported by a sense of agency. It's not a good thing to feel hopeless when so many signs point in this direction. It's not a good thing either to be in denial, and the line is difficult to navigate. There are moments that drive everyone to wonder whether it's time to move on. Until we are sure, we have to take a look at the small moves that are possible, and they may turn out to be larger than imagined. Either way, the healthier road to travel is built on maintaining some vision.

There are still a myriad of choices to make. Students are all different. Regular schedules are interrupted by unpredicted events. How students are encouraged, how they are disciplined, how relationships are built, all these, and the rest of the schoolday's activities are open to a teacher's authentic creative response. Traditional lessons themselves are open to interpretation and nuance. Herein resides the teacher's personal power. Outside of oneself, it's a mistake not to keep the stakeholders in mind, particularly the students. When students are dissatisfied, a teacher has to ask, in what ways have I contributed to their problems? In the long run, the needs of everyone involved within this dynamic system have to be taken into account. For one, the power of the stakeholders has to be reckoned with. Yet, the system is never static, and it's important to notice where choice is available. Empathy is never totally out of reach.

III

Traveling the World

Over the years, we have read about and visited schools in faraway places. The urge to travel was nothing less than the love of adventure, and we were often able to match fortuitously the desire to travel with visits to schools around the world. The travel began with curiosity, but much more happened. It was particularly rewarding to experience people who by their differences had so much to teach us. The common assumptions we hold about what schooling is and how it takes place were delightfully challenged. We saw new possibilities that never had been imagined.

It was especially rewarding to discover that the capacity to establish trust was as great no matter how much we were the same or different. Trust is an integral part of humanistic teaching. Students need to be trusted that under the right conditions they can be highly responsible for their own learning. Trust can open the doors to teacher-student relationships that bring about satisfying and effective teaching and learning on both sides. Our travels demonstrated so well that all over the world there are people who have a deep understanding of humanistic teaching.

- Look for what surprised you in this chapter.
- How do the experiences we describe suggest possibilities for you?
- What is one of your assumptions that has been challenged?
- Which of these places would you most like to visit? Why?

6

In Search of Humanistic Teachers

LIVING IN JAPAN

Dear Dylan,

Did your mom ever tell you about her trip around the world when she was nine? Aunt Simone was six. Heading west, and with only rough plans for many months ahead, the four of us landed in Kyoto in early September 1973. My host at the Kyoto University of Education introduced us to Mr. and Mrs. Inue who had a large home and were willing to rent us three rooms with a kitchen. It didn't have a bathtub, but we would use theirs every other night. It was a traditional house complete with tatami floors (so we didn't wear shoes inside), sliding doors, and a broad veranda that faced a large extraordinary Japanese garden. The house was located in Kowata, a small village about a half-hour away from Kyoto by train. It was a lovely village and a beautiful house.

We ended up living there for three months. Nana made sure that Rachel and Simone were reading, writing, and learning mathematics. My work was to learn about teacher education in Japan, and with Nana to visit local schools. It was convenient that the house we lived in was across from an elementary school. And, there were many trips where we explored Kyoto and the surrounding countryside.

Mr. and Mrs. Inue, or Inuesan as we would address each of them, were a dignified and charming elderly Japanese couple, and they were curious. At their insistence, the six of us would often get together in the evenings, particularly after the four of us would traipse in for our bath night. It was a good thing that we had prepared for the trip by learning to speak Japanese a little, because they spoke no English. Though a long way from fluent, we were able to tell them what we had done during the day. And, they had many suggestions for the next. The conversations were fun and intriguing as we got to know each other. Aunt Simone is one of your favorite people, and so she was for them. Best of all, it wasn't long before we could joke with each other. It was special how close we became. They were very gracious and caring, and we grew to love them.

Before the end of September, Simone broke her leg while she and your mother were playing in the schoolyard across the road. A really bad break. It wasn't a tragedy, but it sure was difficult for her. Reflecting back, it was no surprise how much help the Inuesans gave us. But at the time, it was totally unexpected. With no discussion between us, it began with the presentation of a bedpan the following morning when I brought Simone and Nana back from the hospital. So it went for the next two months as her leg healed. It's hard to imagine not having had their help and caring.

Attention to teacher education and visiting schools went mostly on the back burner. The good part, which could not have been envisioned, was that Nana and I would return to Kyoto, and also visit Kobe, ten years later with an understanding of Japanese culture rooted in a deep personal experience. This knowledge made it possible to take on two projects that actually involved teaching elementary school children and leading a staff development workshop, with the help of a translator, but much on our own. These stories are for another time, but I should at least tell you that we weren't quite ready yet for the insights about humanistic teaching that occurred.

Sayonara was both sad and joyous as we left for Taiwan. We only stayed there for a week, but we have fond memories of visiting the National Palace Museum in Taipei twice. It was profound how the artifacts represented a totally different view of human history than we have in the West. This was what our trip was about—to see our lives in perspective, in general and as educators. Of course, Chinese culture itself was teaching us so much, although we had fewer opportunities for learning there than we had in Japan, but still provocative. And, there was the striking contrast between Japanese and Chinese cultures.

From there, for another short stay, we flew to Hong Kong. Here was another way of experiencing life in China, plus one event that made a big difference over the next three months. We met two social workers from New York who were also traveling west around the world, Nancy Duggan and Denis McCrae. Since they too were headed for Bangkok, we decided to meet there and travel together for awhile. Denis was a photographer who focused on people. Nancy had lived in Thailand when she was in the Peace Corps, and she had learned to speak Thai. Nancy has become like a great aunt to you, but chances are that you don't know this about her. They were both interested in visiting schools, and our adventures took on new dimensions. We all were excited. By now, your mother and your aunt had become a year older.

Soon after arriving in Bangkok, I firmed up plans for a visit to Chulalongkorn University in Khon Kaen, in central Thailand about 100 miles due north. Before we left the States, I was told they had an unusual humanistic school there, with open classrooms, and visiting there was on the top of my list. However, it would be more convenient, I was told, if we could arrive in two or three weeks, not right away. Because there was so much to see and do in Bangkok, including visiting a few schools, this was no delay. Staying on at the Atlanta Hotel, popular among low-budget world travelers, with a beautiful pool surrounded by palm trees, was easy.

But once again our plans changed. Travelers coming back from Vientiane had extraordinary stories to tell. With the war in Vietnam recently over, people were now traveling to Laos that for so long had been unsafe to visit. There was an overnight train to the border that departed most every evening. All we had to do when we arrived was to find a ferry that would transport us across the Mekong River. Vientiane was not too far by cab from the landing on the Laotian side. Why not? A week later, the six of us boarded the night train that would take us on beyond Khon Kaen, to where we would return on the way back. We had already thought we were traveling to remote places in the world, but on the train we had even less of an inkling of what to expect.

Now comes the part of the story that sounds like a fairy tale. We weren't in Vientiane for much more than a week, when travelers from further up north returned with their tales of Luang Prabang, the ancient capitol of Laos, where the king was currently in residence. There was a small plane that flew there a few times a week, and we were told it was safe to go there as long as we didn't try to travel overland. A week later, definitely traveling north and not west for the time being, there we were, our small band of explorers, in a small town with one telephone, in a delightful mostly outdoor hotel, in three "rooms" that were barely four walls atop a concrete slab, and a restaurant that was simply tables under umbrellas. Nancy's knowledge of Thai was close enough to understand and speak some Laotian. With this advantage, after going to the morning market where we could have bought an armadillo to cook for our dinner, we were off to find a school.

*   *   *

Picture a class of elementary students sitting in rows in a wooden room, low to the ground, one of four attached end to end to make a large rectangle with walls in-between where the blackboards hang.

Screens slightly separate the rest of the room from the outdoors. A wide overhang on all sides keeps out the rain, when it comes. Just beyond the door to the classroom is a children's garden—covering more land than the school itself. Inside, there are rows of benches with bench-like desks, each making room for six students. And, each is a little higher than the next on a slanted floor. Down in the front is the teacher who is aiming a pointer at Laotian letters and words. Young students are reciting them in chorus. However different, the impression is one of a school that is not considerably far from the ordinary.

We were standing in the doorway, half outdoors, quietly watching a lesson in progress. Always a teacher, your nana has a well-honed ability to understand what is going on in a classroom, even when she doesn't speak the language. She figured out that a little boy quite close to us, at the back of the room on the end of the highest bench, was unsuccessfully searching for a pencil. She opened her bag, found one, and reaching up, quietly handed it to him. At one point, I wondered how many students there were in this class. It looked crowded, but somehow different than other crowded classrooms I'd seen. I counted, caught my breath, and nudged your Nana. I whispered, do you realize that there are eighty children in this room? Three benches wide, five or six on each, and five rows back. She counted and nodded. We looked at each other. These youngsters were sitting so close together, it wasn't obvious at first. Wow! They sure are attentive. Afterwards, with Nancy's help, we talked with the teacher for a short while.

*   *   *

What we saw and heard made us realize that for these children, this was an unusual experience. School was a rare privilege. The garden helped to make it practical, because the students could bring home needed food for their families. In this traditional Laotian school, there was none of the commotion expected in a crowded classroom. Indeed, there was none of the commotion we saw in regular schools in Kyoto or Bangkok. The kids sat beaming while listening or reciting lessons about letters, words, and numbers. Paying attention was their only reality. This was serious business for little people, and they knew it. This was their window to a different world. These weren't crowded conditions. School was a magical opportunity that satisfied their almost unimaginable needs. Just so, the teacher felt that her greatest hopes were being fulfilled.

We wondered how this classroom, so much like those everywhere, was in our eyes a humanistic classroom. This is the way it felt. Maybe a fairy tale can sometimes be real. Another time, more adventures.

With much love, Grangran

So, when we arrived in Khon Kaen a couple of weeks later, by comparison, even though the school was completely unlike others we had seen, it seemed normal. The school had a lot of outdoors, but the buildings were substantial. The building that housed the combination auditorium and lunchroom was in the open air, but a huge roof cantilevered out over the entire space. In the classrooms, children were not sitting in rows, unlike what we had seen everywhere else. They were engaged in learning by themselves, in small groups, and sometimes all sitting together. Some were sitting on the floor and some on chairs. Occasionally, they sat around group tables to participate together in a discussion with the whole class. There was always more than one teacher. Sometimes teachers were just moving around ready to offer help, and other times, they taught lessons and led activities.

Dean Saisuree Chutikul headed the Department of Education at Khon Kaen University. Dean Saisuree, as she was known, had been educated at the University of Indiana in the 1960s and while there, she noticed that the open classroom schools in the United States had a resemblance to the way education took place for centuries in the temple courtyards—called *watt* schools. Regular schools in Thailand were copied from the West, just as they were in Japan. Her experimental program, she argued, was rooted in Thai culture. In good part for this reason, she felt it was succeeding.

It's not that everything happening in this school was happening smoothly. Teachers were interviewed, and they revealed a share of difficulties. The students, their parents, and the teachers found themselves in a world where many of the typical norms of school were absent. Gone were the rules that played their expected role for keeping order in the day-to-day business of school. As they improvised their actions in this new environment, they struggled at times. Yet, they expressed optimism for what they thought was a valuable educational experiment.

From our observations, class activities often resulted in high levels of participation and on-task classroom work. One could see many kinds of support and challenge coming from the teachers and in return from the students. Even if the teachers were struggling, they certainly were cheery. They looked liked they were enjoying their work. The students clearly enjoyed learning in an environment that offered many more degrees of freedom than other schools we would visit. And, they must have known from past experience or from other children what other schools were like. Like the Laotian children we observed in Luang Prabang, the teachers and students were responding to school as an adventure.

Our experiences were too limited to say whether most Thai and Laotian children regarded school learning in and of itself as an adventure. In these two cases, though, both the teachers and the students were exploring territories that were unfamiliar to them. The journey beckoned them into the unknown. It generated an excitement that was palpable. From our idealistic and myopic point of view, both of these examples focused too much on ordinary achievement. From another view, teachers and students were being challenged to broaden their horizons in ways that connected them to each other and to a bigger world.

Prajaub Thirabutana (1971) wrote about the ways her horizons were broadened and how she was pushed to connect to the great, wide world. She grew up in the backwoods of Thailand, so remote that little was heard of the outside world. With the coming of the roads, villagers ancient in their ways discovered wonders they had never imagined. They also discovered that they were poor. They had problems—so difficult at times—but this problem they didn't have before. Thirabutana came to Bangkok in the 1950s, succeeded in becoming a teacher, and with encouragement from one of her teachers, wrote about her childhood. In the end, new horizons are often desired. But, the quality of life we achieve is still of our own making in the old world or the new. Our experiences offered us unusual perspectives. We still feel privileged that the people we met became a part of our lives. Our world of education was greatly enlarged.

TOMOE: A HUMANISTIC SCHOOL IN TOKYO

One school we couldn't visit was Tomoe, which had been located in southwest Tokyo in the years between 1937 and 1945, before it burned to the ground as a result of Allied bombing. Almost as unlikely as traveling there was the school itself. Reminiscent of the Summerhill School in England already established in the 1920s, Tomoe was equally radical within the context of Japanese culture.

The school was unknown to most people until its history was brought to light in the early 1980s in a book by Tetsuko Kuroyanagi (1982), first in Japanese and a year later in an English translation. Coming across the book while in Tokyo in 1984, Gene Stivers, a colleague from Temple, decided it would be an ideal gift for Donna, given that she taught at Project Learn and had herself recently returned from Japan. *Totto-chan*, as it was entitled, was Kuroyanagi's nickname when she enrolled in first grade at Tomoe around the onset of World War II. The school is brought to life with stories told through her eyes as a child. We were touched by her writing and amazed to discover a school like this in Japan, whenever in history. We had returned a year earlier from Kobe, and our second visit to Kyoto, so we knew that there was present-day interest. But surprisingly, we now saw that this interest in humanistic teaching was more widespread, beyond our imagination. Astonishingly the book had sold four and a half million copies in the one year before it was translated into English.

Amazed, surprised, and astonished describe Kuroyanagi's reaction as well. Already a famous host and interviewer on Japanese national television, she was accustomed to large audiences and acclaim. But her interest in writing the book, which required significant encouragement, stemmed from the humbler goal of a promise made to the headmaster, Sosaku Kobayashi, while she was a student at Tomoe. He had founded Tomoe as a place to express his humanistic philosophy of education—acquired over years of study and travel. So appreciative was Totto-chan that one day she said, "I'd like to teach at this school when I grow up. I really would." Instead of smiling, he responded in all seriousness, "Promise?" Totto-chan vigorously nodded her head and added, "I promise" (pp. 178–179). Though Kobayashi lived until 1963, he never succeeded in rebuilding the school nor did he ever write its story. Clearly, the debt has been paid in full, and he would have been especially proud, because in large measure Kuroyanagi's experiences at Tomoe contributed to the success of this venture and her life as a whole.

Behind the promise is the fact that Totto-chan has the distinction of being expelled from first grade. She had disrupted her class at her old school too many times, including jumping out of her seat to get a look at the street musicians who were passing by, from which came the subtitle: *The Little Girl at the Window.* (Wisely, her mother didn't tell her this until she was an adult.) With little fuss, her mother simply told her that she was going to a new school. What they found were classrooms housed in six retired railway cars, with the regular seats removed and the overhead bins left in place for storing coats and book bags.

Who they found in the office was Mr. Kobayashi, a man with abundant patience, an interest in listening, and an educational plan that centered on children's needs. After a short time to insure that Totto-chan was comfortable, her mother was sent home and the two of them began talking. Sitting close, across from each other, Mr. Kobayashi said, "Now then, tell me all about yourself. Tell me anything at all you want to talk about" (p. 32). When the little girl paused, he asked if there was anything else. And, they spoke from morning until lunchtime. It's easy to see the beginnings of her later success.

The possibility of this conversation fits well within the overall philosophy. The mornings were dedicated to the regular lessons of any school, but the children worked most of the time on their own—choosing the order of their studies as suited them. The afternoons were open to walking, observing nature, collecting plants, sketching, playing music, and occasionally listening to short talks from the headmaster. His aim was to have a curriculum that was sufficiently free to support the development of individuality and self-respect, turning the traditional high regard for respect in Japan into self-respect. The students were encouraged to find what interested them in the formal and informal studies, and the teachers were encouraged to improvise their lessons around what unfolded. The overall structure of activities was carefully thought out to achieve particular goals, but this included the contributions of the children's work and play. Kobayashi believed that most learning for children takes care of itself in a stimulating environment, and he was known to say, "Don't cramp their ambitions. Their dreams are bigger than yours" (p. 16). He worried about too much adult interference.

Music played a large role in the school program. Kobayashi had studied eurythmics with Emile Jaques-Delcroze in Paris in the 1920s. He integrated music activities daily, particularly those with attention to rhythm, to address his concern for balanced growth of the mind and the body. He found too much emphasis on the written word troublesome. Equally, there was a need to heighten sensual perception and intuitive receptiveness—much like the extensive art program that is joined with many of the subjects at Project Learn. These same concerns motivated not only music but the time spent on learning outdoors, regular field trips, and the incorporation of participation in community events. Still, he would regularly engage children in the importance of words—like the time he introduced public speaking at lunchtime in the assembly hall, where students took turns on different days telling the other students and their teachers "about something." However the children were challenged, they were sure to be pushed. At the same time, there were always loopholes to insure that each child could find adequate support. Like music, finding balance in every moment was basic to the teaching at Tomoe.

Kobayashi spoke of a still small voice of God that for him was the foundation of inspiration. Hearts that are never moved, so never being set on fire, is what he feared. And, Kuroyanagi grew up knowing this well. It's easy to believe about her first eventful year, when Totto-chan says, "she had eagerly looked forward to every single morning of it" (p. 133). It's understandable too to believe Donna when she talks about teaching at Project Learn, "There were no end of problems, but I looked forward to each day as I left home in the morning for school." There is a hokeyness about these expressions of praise, but recognizing the truth carried within them sets a valuable benchmark about the nature of good education.

THE CHALLENGE TO BE HUMANISTIC IN JAPAN AND THE SOVIET UNION

In 1983, we traveled again to Japan, first to Kobe to teach elementary school students mental imagery techniques for studying English. From Kobe, we returned to the Kyoto University of Education, where we had visited ten years before, to lead a teacher education workshop on Gestalt theory and practice. Three years later, in 1986, we were invited by the Soviet Academy of Pedagogical Sciences to lead, together with three of our colleagues, a two-day seminar on humanistic education. Before we returned home, we flew a thousand miles south of Moscow to visit T'bilisi and an extraordinary public elementary school, resembling Project Learn writ large, in the then Soviet Republic of Georgia.

Back then, it was the joy of travel that highlighted these trips. In retrospect, we can attribute to them significant aspects of how our perspective has broadened over the years. Humanistic teaching, hardly impractical, can be woven into education in ways that seem at first beyond ken.

Kobe: Teaching Imagery Techniques

One of the studies in *Imagery in Teaching and Learning* (Allender, 1991) was carried out in two Japanese elementary schools in Kobe. The students we met were part of an after-school enrichment program. A colleague, Professor Yoshia Kurato at Kobe University, was interested in the application of mental imagery techniques to classroom learning and kindly made the arrangements and served as translator. In studies with American children, the scope of the research included the teaching of vocabulary, spelling, arithmetic, writing, and Russian language lessons. In Japan, we adapted five imagery exercises for the teaching of English.

Over the period of a week, the children were delighted with exercises that required writing with their eyes closed, learning words by their shape, turning the meaning of words into pictures, associating vocabulary words with textures, and mentally placing them into imaginary flags that were described in a guided fantasy. Asking the children to write with their eyes closed drew giggles, but altogether the students were as cooperative and engaged as any teacher could wish. Only once, when Donna was leading a discussion and the children began talking out of turn, did she have to raise her voice slightly. The children startled and immediately paid attention, even before her words were translated. With knowing smiles from the students, and from Donna, the lesson continued in the fun way it had been going all along.

Normally, the structure of these classes was more traditional, but there was no hint that the introduction of creative methods of teaching was disruptive for the students or their teachers who were present. Nor was it expected. We were not making changes in the normal structure; we were simply exploring the use of methods that leave more room for students to match their individual styles of learning with the lessons that were being presented—in our terms, to better meet their individual needs. We observed a positive response, and this fit with the children's success on short tests and what their teachers observed about their learning. The result was no different than what had taken place with American children attending the Project Learn School.

There was no evidence for grand conclusions, but enough to produce some insights. In a radically different cultural context, it was possible to practice some aspect of our humanistic teaching without upsetting the comfort that students and their teachers had grown to expect in their daily classroom context. These students profited from the changes, at least in the moment, and maybe the teachers and the students actually shifted a little in the long run. Certainly, we demonstrated an unfamiliar manner of teaching and learning. Their excitement and ours spoke to other possibilities, in other contexts— even more germane within our own culture. Whenever and wherever teachers introduce creative teaching methods, there is the likelihood that children's needs are being better met. Providing students with a humanistic teacher might require no more than recognizing how much creativity is already happening at times, for anyone of us, and building on the strength of what we already have been doing. Children in traditional educational environments can profit from changes, even small ones, just as children in classrooms who have the advantage of many more degrees of freedom.

Kyoto: A Gestalt Workshop for Teachers

Besides the wonder of staying again at the Inue home in Kowata, we had the pleasure of leading a day-long teacher education workshop at the Kyoto University of Education with preservice teachers who were making a career change and some of their college professors, ten participants in all. Professor Nishi Nishinosono, who had been our host in the 1970s, arranged the workshop, but in this case a translator wasn't necessary. The participants were fluent in English to different degrees, and among them, they were able to decipher what we were saying when there was confusion. Besides, much of the workshop involved experiential activities, and at these times, the teachers spoke Japanese among themselves. Not anticipating this, it seemed momentarily that this was a disadvantage, because we couldn't listen in on the small groupings that constantly reformed for each short experience we had planned. In contrast, our ability to notice the emotional quality of their interactions was heightened and proved to be a boon to our leadership.

The focus was on teacher-student interactions and the mix of teachers and students also proved to be an advantage, itself heightening the verisimilitude of our conversations. In planning the workshop, concerns had been raised about the norms of Japanese culture that ran counter to a highly interactive workshop design. And indeed, early on, when we asked them to form pairs and spend four or five minutes sharing their strengths in turn, there was an initial reluctance. Timidity, even. The exercise probably seemed too much like bragging and impolite; yet, there was also a counter pressure about not following a teacher's instructions, also impolite. In fact, what soon followed was energetic engagement. And amidst their slightly raised voices and laughter, we too felt the loss of being unsure. Together, we tackled problems of conflicting expectations, what we call internalized "shoulds," the experience of careful listening, and the productive expression of resentments and appreciations.

We weren't yet aware of *Totto-chan*, then already in print and popular, and no one mentioned it. Therefore, we don't know if the book had any influence on their receptivity to the concepts that were demonstrated that day. It was initially made clear, however, that none of the participants had a particular interest in humanistic education. On the other hand, they were all eager to explore innovative ways of thinking about teaching and delighted to have an opportunity to learn some new ideas from two American teachers. It helped too when they learned that we had visited the university and had lived in Kowata ten years ago.

What joined us was our humanity, and so we touched each other. Reflecting on the experience of leading this workshop, there is no doubt we learned just as they did. Our audience was special in the sense that each person wanted to be a teacher or already was a teacher of teachers. Not only were they eager to learn, they were like many of the people with whom we worked back home. Many with whom we taught at Temple University and Project Learn were predisposed to support humanistic concepts, but many others were not. Not only did we find students in Kobe who could easily appreciate our ideals about education, we found teachers there equally responsive. Once again, our learning was enhanced by the cultural difference. The ease of teaching in Kobe and of leading the workshop pointed toward underlying needs of students and teachers everywhere that warrant special attention. The overall message says something about the opportunities that may lay hidden from us—but not so much that they would be too difficult to decode—as a path to the improvement of teaching.

Moscow: Small Group Discussions in an Amphitheater

As active members of the Association of Humanistic Psychology (AHP), we were invited in 1984 by Fran Macy, who headed the AHP Soviet Project, to join a delegation to the Soviet Union to meet with interested psychologists and educators. For forgotten reasons, probably having to do with money, only Jerry went. The grand purpose, likely to fail, was to take part in an effort to reduce tensions between the Soviets and the Americans. The Cold War was in full force, and the threat of worldwide nuclear destruction was palpable. Daily life went on, but there was a pervasive air of dread while the two countries lined up ballistic missiles aimed at each other. No one on the planet could reasonably imagine immunity to the potential destruction. In response, it was not uncommon during the 1980s for activists in various professions to join small groups of citizen diplomats. We wanted to do something practical to soften the belligerence and the despair in spite of how hopeless the effort might seem.

The trip was exciting. Thirty Americans traveled to Leningrad, Moscow, and T'bilisi for two weeks of visits to universities, clinics, and schools. Though there were significant theoretical differences, observations and discussions of practices in the field found many similarities. We all aimed toward humane, helpful psychology and high quality education as if we were on the same team. Tensions arising from a need to be mortal enemies were nonexistent, and on both sides, the political posturing was regarded as wasteful and foolish. The friendship experienced, the ideas exchanged, and the active observation of ongoing programs all together enhanced everyone's knowledge—judging from our shared enthusiasm. In parting, we hoped that this would not be the last opportunity to meet, but a beginning.

There was then no great surprise when we were invited a second time to join the delegation in 1986, the fourth since 1983. However, what was surprising was a request for the two of us to plan a two-day seminar with members of the Moscow Academy of Pedagogical Sciences. An opportunity like this wasn't to be turned down, and what little resistance we had disappeared when the Soviets wanted to learn about humanistic education. Plus, if one could imagine the need for anything else, two weeks before we would arrive, Carl Rogers (e.g., 1951, 1969, 1983) was scheduled to speak and demonstrate his methods of teaching and facilitating groups. We were going to be Act II and felt honored to be on the program.

Planning turned out to be problematic, but not at first. It was spring when we invited Lucy Miller, Morgan Henderson, and Nancy Aronson, three educators from Philadelphia with whom we had worked, to become an American team of five. And, we looked forward to meeting with Irina Dubrovina who was, within the Moscow Academy, the deputy director of the Institute for General and Educational Psychology. She would be in Washington, D.C., during the summer. When we finally arrived in Moscow in the fall, we would meet again with her and also with Alexei Matyushkin, the director of the institute.

Our goal was to have a conference, reflecting Rogerian theory that modeled two presentations, one about the Project Learn School and the other an example of doing action research in a Philadelphia public school. To demonstrate the principles, we proposed to have our delegation and an equal number of Soviets working in six small groups. The presentations were to take place in an initial plenary session, followed by four two-hour work meetings of about ten each, balanced for the two countries, with a facilitator, and one or two translators (ideally one of theirs and one of ours). The seminar would close with a final plenary session to discuss what we had learned. The task of the small groups was to discuss over two days the presentations in terms of agreed-upon themes leading to personally relevant applications, shared concerns, and unsolved problems. The meeting in Washington went well, a correspondence with Matyushkin was initiated, and some minor changes because of technical difficulties were ironed out and agreed upon.

Our gut reaction at the start of the meeting in Moscow several days before the conference was not good. We seemed to have been naïve and unsuspecting. Slowly, we came to understand Matyushkin's special needs. Rogers had been a first-rate hit, but the program had been limited to sixty members of the Academy of Psychological

Sciences. Matyushkin was under great pressure to allow any member of the academy who wanted to attend, as many as 300. Scheduling now limited the time for the small groups and the number to four, because there weren't enough translators. The "small" groups might have more than seventy-five participants each, and we thought we heard that there had to be formal presentations from many of the Soviets. What was unfolding did not in any way reflect the highly interactive seminar we had envisioned. It seemed that the conference was turning into an ordinary talk show, without the humor.

Confronting the problems, we remembered the good will that had been present all through the planning process. We agreed easily on four topics: humanistic teaching, humanistic research, creativity, and psychological services. We heard clearly that the Soviets as well thought that the reading of formal papers would be deadly. It stood that Matyushkin wanted everyone to hear about Project Learn, the methods of action research, and future scenarios. It stood that a high proportion of the time would be devoted to small group discussions; brief Soviet presentations would be inserted where they made relevant contributions to the discussion. The Soviets' priority was an open exchange of ideas, thus matching the essence of our design. Matyushkin clarified that the plan was a serious departure from the norm, and for him, this was the humanistic cutting edge.

Oddly, it was the plenary sessions that stole the show. The success of the small groups was seen in vibrant, enlightening discussions. But more dramatically, the same can be said about the plenary sessions with a final count of 200 in attendance. In the minutes before the opening of the conference, we were shocked to find ourselves in a cavernous hall shaped like a Greek amphitheater but indoors where high ceilings blocked the sky and the ascending tiers were stuffed with high-backed wooden benches running the length of every row. A shelf attached to the benches ran along the backside and served as a narrow desktop for those above. All this was rising to the rafters where one looked down to a faraway stage. We were sure that Socrates never taught on a stage like this, and yet with great cooperation we stimulated a dialogue worthy of the Greek philosophers. As part of the presentation, no one seemed to mind when we asked them on several occasions to form small groups of five or six by joining with the people in back of them, talking uphill and downhill about questions that were being raised.

Evaluating the conference, we now understood that the Soviets' interest in humanistic education reflected a body of research that they had accumulated over many years. True enough, their need to interconnect their findings with Marxist theory clouded our vision of the overlap. Professor A. V. Petrovsky, who was a participant, gifted us with his book, *Studies in Psychology: The Collective and the Individual* (1985), published in Moscow and translated only the year before. We saw the influences of Lev Semyonovich Vygostsky, who is well known in the West today, and others like Alexander Romanovich Luria and A. N. Leontiev. They were focused on the critical role that group processes played, not only in the functioning of a collective, but in how learning takes place as well. Furthermore, oppression was not part of their vocabulary when it comes to educating children; as teachers, they were concerned about the development of mutually supportive relationships. They understood the vital role of the individual in the functioning of a group. In inviting us, they were looking for affirmation and new horizons.

There is a story of Rogers asking the minister of education why he was invited to talk about his views of group processes, individualized instruction, and creativity. He went on to ask, "Isn't this somewhat dangerous to do in a collective society?" The answer he got was, "Yes, but not as dangerous as not doing it" (Vasconcellos, 1987, p. 7). We witnessed courage, and as much, the ordinary behavior of teachers and teacher educators. We were in a foreign land, and at the end, it was hardly foreign at all. We realized that this extraordinary experience conveyed a simple truth. It is the unwarranted assumptions and the lack of imagination that limits our abilities and the meaning of *realistic*—in matters of educating children, no less than any matters of our lives.

T'bilisi: A Humanistic School in Soviet Georgia

Experimental School Number One in T'bilisi, Georgia, had 2,500 students. They were working in small groups. They were painting pictures and murals on paper taped to the walls of the hallway. They were working on science experiments. And the teachers were moving about listening and helping and showing as needed, sometimes teaching small groups and sometimes teaching the whole class. What an amazing shock and delight we had when we entered this most unique and unusual school in the then Soviet Union. The other schools we visited were pleasant but usual with children in rows and teachers in front of the class. Here in Number One there were children all over though their chairs were in rows and sometimes their teachers were in front of the class teaching a lesson. The feeling of the school was that choosing a project, working with a classmate, and finding a comfortable space in which to work was the norm. Upon entering the school, we felt we were in a vastly expanded version of Project Learn.

The charismatic head of the school, Dr. S. A. Amanashvilli, created this school as a model for education. He was the head of an educational research program in the Institute of Psychology in the Georgian Academy of Sciences, in T'bilisi, interconnected with the Moscow Academy of Pedagogical Sciences. He spoke animatedly about education and what it should be like and what it should accomplish. After our day in the school, our Philadelphia group and others joined him for dinner and talked well into the night. It was not surprising by the time we parted we were all in close agreement about the possibilities of schools and what schooling should be.

One of the very special events of that day was watching Dr. Amanashvilli teach a class of six-year-old children. In addition to being a visionary leader, he was a master teacher. It was not his amazing variety of teaching methods that most impressed us. Rather, it was how he was working with the children on math problems. He asked them to close their eyes while holding up their hands with correct answers to problems he had written on the board. He then moved from child to child indicating that their answer was correct by touching their hand or gently changing an incorrect answer by changing the number of fingers a child was holding up. In this lesson, he demonstrated his fundamental humanism, his concern for each child. No one was shamed by an error. Everyone was acknowledged for the work he or she was doing.

Not all the teachers we observed had the energy of Dr. Amanashvilli, but each one had a special way with the children. Of course we realized these teachers knew they were part of an unusual experiment in the Soviet Union and expected to be observed. The teachers at Project Learn also regularly find themselves with parents or other visitors most days of the week. This does tend to make them keenly aware of what and how they are teaching. The teachers at School Number One were gracious and very interested in the work we were doing in the United States. They were pleased to hear that we shared common ways of educating our children.

We saw many connections with Project Learn. Neither Project Learn nor Number One relies on grades as the evaluation of students' progress—a source of discomfort for many parents. They spoke about the need to affirm each child's development and the negative effects of comparing children to each other. Their goal as members of a collective society was to have the best efforts of each person available to the group, and they felt this was best achieved by allowing each person to develop her or his abilities and interests. Though Project Learn lives in a capitalist society, it too values the importance of the individual's contribution to the group as critical to a humanistic education.

It was clear that both these schools required a lot of time and energy of their teachers. Yet all of them relished the opportunity to teach and learn in such exciting and stimulating environments. We recognized that as educators we have a job to do with parents who are fearful and unsure when children are given choices about their learning and not given grades. We agreed that an important part of the teacher's job in both schools is the reeducation of all the adults, ourselves included. The success of humanistic education depends on trusting an innovative curriculum and knowing that a child's progress is not judged in comparison with the work of others. Parents, teachers, and students, we understood, all need to learn to trust their own good judgment in looking at the data, the students' work. Most parents of School Number One's children were actively supportive of the school and its philosophy. They welcomed the innovative programs without being afraid that their children were not getting enough of the regular subjects. They valued their children's enthusiasm for going to school and how lively they were about their studies.

IV

The Academic Context

Academic scholarship has made a significant contribution to our work as teachers. The hegemony of science was replaced by a partnership forged by humanistic research, and educational theory generated in this way was easily put into practice. Moreover, the development and acceptance of self-study research methodologies, a recent innovation, made way for academics and teachers in general to feel that their expertise was, though from different angles, truly on par. Nothing more could have better placed both parties in the position of doing similar work and enhancing their common understandings of teaching and learning processes. None of these efforts alone has resulted in large shifts in how schooling takes place, but all of the work together reveals significant humanistic change since mid-twentieth century. A worthy accomplishment.

Typically, teachers do not have a high regard for the contribution that educational research can make to their practice. There are conditions in place today that might shift this attitude positively to a meaningful degree. Research is work, and time is limited. Still, when the research process overlaps the daily tasks of teaching, there are practical opportunities to combine the two. For us, the task is like mining; if there is a bit of gold to find, the time can often be found. Surely, difficult social conditions will overwhelm any amount of rewarding effort, but with this humbling awareness, our lives are enriched by the small differences we make each day.

- What elements of the following chapters encourage you about the value of research for your own teaching?

- What aspect of your own practice as a teacher would you be interested in studying?
- How does our notion of global impact boost your hopefulness or support your skepticism?
- Formulate a research question that you would like to pursue with collaborators: other teachers, professors, parents, or someone else.

7
The Possibility of Humanistic Research

What is required is a firm but playful embrace of otherness, of counter-culture research assumptions, of stepping out of a comfortable research paradigm with attendant theories and into an uncomfortable one, even if for only as long as it takes to finish reading a helpfully disquieting book.

—Bullough, Jr., 2006, p. 5

UNBOLTING THE SCIENTIFIC FRAMEWORK

Juxtaposing the two words *humanistic* and *research* appears to be an oxymoron. For most of the twentieth century this would have been so. Humanistic actions require close attention to the ongoing needs of the individual person; the history of scholarly research had grown to mean rising above these needs in a search for a more general truth. The terms precluded each other, because their contradictory meanings at best derived from different spheres of concerns and action. In 1978, Ian Mitroff and Ralph Kilmann, two social scientists in the field of business, challenged this assumption. They proposed an alternative to the solidified research framework that had become the traditional and revered canon. Based on a Jungian framework, they proposed a classification of research methods that encompassed a wide range of intellectual and emotional processes that guide human behavior. Combinations of sensing, thinking, intuition, and feeling were matched with four approaches to research—framed as an analytic scientist, a conceptual theorist, a conceptual humanist, and a particular humanist. Though their terms never became popular, Mitroff and Kilmann were among the first of a growing number of scholars to begin unbolting the scientific framework.

The following decade (cf. Denzin and Lincoln, 1994) was an exciting time for researchers who worried that there was too little attention given to humanistic concerns. The history of the development of alternative research methods sometimes goes further back, but this was when their energetic and wide-scale development began. Granted, it wasn't easy to find a supportive professional environment in which to do this kind of research. Still, what resulted in the long run was the establishment of a vigorous field of qualitative research methods, in addition to the quantitative ones that characterized the traditional scientific paradigm. The hegemony of the traditional canon has never disappeared, as evidenced by the ubiquitous testing of schoolchildren, but humanistic influences have succeeded in occupying a strong position within the academy. And for educational research, as elsewhere, the field continues to grow. Its articulate voices maintain a humanistic vision, which parallels and often mirrors everyday practices in the classroom.

The traditional canon and the newer qualitative methods seem to each have their place. The dichotomy also keeps scholars aware of the ever-present tension between theory and practice. The results of traditional research designs are less likely to find ready application than qualitative studies. There is a prevalence of research that cannot readily be applied—particularly frustrating for classroom teachers. Sometimes, teachers are blamed—for their lack of skill in the interpretation of research or faltering interest. Placing the fault with teachers, however, is no more reasonable than blaming students for their failure to learn. The responsibility for either is a two-sided affair. Unnoticed is how the results of research designs that are the most tightly controlled for "extraneous" variables are the least likely to offer results that make sense to a teacher. And its opposite, the more a study is a product of the usual everyday classroom myriad of tensions and surprises, the chance is higher that it will be of interest and useful. There is no question that theory is important, but tending to the balance of theory and practice has helped to bring about greater attention to neglected humanistic concerns.

For so many years, it had been presumed that the development of teaching skills was best accomplished by learning and applying experimentally established facts—which ignored the ever-present subjective side to a teacher's daily work. Forget about the needs of the students for the moment. The avant-garde that better addressed the practical problems of teachers was well represented in *Human Inquiry: A Sourcebook of New Paradigm Research* edited by Peter

Reason and John Rowan in 1981. Efforts were made to lessen the hegemonic effects of science with proposals for designs that meant engaging in mutually respectful conversations among all the participants in a research project—research that itself challenged other kinds of social power. An overarching theme was collaboration, what was called collaborative research that might involve an array of stakeholders, not as subjects, but as participants. What emerged was renewed interest in action research. The methods involved the creation of community among the participants whose common task was to explore problems in classrooms and schools. There were opportunities to discuss and modify the methods, contribute to the data pool, take active part in interpreting the data, and brainstorm creative actions for solving problems. Throughout *Human Inquiry*, very much a sourcebook, discussions about validity of research had as their starting points the needs of practitioners.

Peter Elbow (1986) pointed to the blinding potency of what he called a "methodology of doubt" that ruled scientific research. It is not only that hypotheses are assumed to be false unless proven otherwise, there is an underlying assumption that people are unlikely to be truthful. What is left out is the trust that must be established for honest interchange. Elbow argued that there was an equal and balancing need for a "methodology of belief" that can be used to shape both teaching and research. With hindsight we can see that modern-day research was based on a climate of distrust, not unlike what exists in most schools. In the academic world, so often, people's experience is ground down to numbers and theorized with jargon-laden language. Irrespective of subjects' feelings, how this has colored the verisimilitude of the data is ignored. Not all such research is bad, but its importance certainly has to be tempered with this perspective. Elbow asked us, both as students and as researchers, to consider appropriate times for making an effort to believe that there is some kind of useful truth in whatever another person has to say.

Empathy is needed in the service of understanding the context of others. Elbow (1986) designed a "believing game" with guidelines that assisted an exploration of the substance and details of other points of view. For example, it is useful to identify many instances where agreement might be possible. At one level, this is a search for common understandings. Interpersonally, it is a method for building relationships and fostering collaboration. On another level, the goal is to expose the context within which the other functions, especially where interpersonal relationships are not present—as in text. There are cultural contexts that differentially affect how intellect and emotion are expressed. Carol Gilligan (1982) made this point clearly with dramatic examples of girls and women who had been generally misrepresented, because no account was taken for how they speak, in her terms, "in a different voice." Whether as a teaching or research methodology, the thrust is in the direction of a broader understanding of whom we teach or study. There is no commitment to agree with what one has come to understand; the aim is to be in a position to make judgments as to its worth and relevance.

The benefit to prospective teachers was finding in their academic education more professors who worked at bringing theory and practice closer together. The classroom environments in colleges of education for learning about teaching steadily were becoming more in tune with progressive thought. With the idea that educational research is more realistically conceived as a personal and social process (Allender, 1986), worries about needing to be born a teacher were replaced with greater optimism that teaching skills can be learned. Though a teacher education student might not have noticed these changes consciously, there was an excitement in teacher education circles that was palpable. Problematically, some professors needed to assert the wisdom of traditional scientific research, protecting themselves from the vulnerability that is experienced when radical change is occurring. But no doubt, the knowledge needed to be a good teacher was no longer the same. When the second edition of the *Introduction to Qualitative Research Methods* by Steven Taylor and Robert Bogdan (1984) was published, it was subtitled, *The Search for Meanings*. Truth was taking a backseat to meaning, and for professors who had some support or a slight excess of courage, the academic community was transforming itself into a more inclusive locus of dialogue.

Other significant signs of unbolting the scientific framework appeared within this climate of change. Further from the basic notion of establishing a problem to be investigated, a method of collecting and analyzing data, and drawing conclusions and implications, the idea that the writing of stories should be included within the pale of academic research was born with the name *Narrative Psychology* (Sarbin, 1986). As a methodology that was focused on the creation of meaning, it had its own unique techniques. But here too, the meaning of human experiences was detailed and interpreted with the possibility of drawing conclusions and suggesting implications.

And, it wasn't long before it was proposed that the broad conception of many if not all art forms could be included within the framework of potentially valid investigative methods. In 1991, Elliot Eisner published *The Enlightened Eye*, expanding qualitative inquiry into the realm of arts-based research for the enhancement of educational practice. He argued that the traditions of art criticism could be brought to bear for assaying the quality of research. Today, both story writing in particular and the arts in general are vibrant aspects of educational research—providing explicit and implicit support for their place in education at all levels. The humanities and the role of humanistic teaching practices found their natural connection.

It was in this same period that Donald Schön (1983, 1987) explored the space where theory and practice meet, and by blurring this space, he ended up showing how the two can strengthen each other. In his words, "the question of the relationship between practice competence and professional knowledge needs to be turned upside down. We should start not by asking how to make better use of research-based knowledge but by asking what we can learn from a careful examination of artistry, that is, the competence of which practitioners actually handle indeterminate zones of practice—however that competence may relate to technical rationality" (Schön, 1987, p. 13). Using a process that requires systematic reflection on one's own practice, with attention to the specifics, a teacher can expect to hone skills for working on classroom problems in ways that lead to effective new behaviors.

Schön's key concept was "reflection-in-action." Ordinarily, there are many routinized responses in moment-to-moment acts of teaching. And often, we are surprised by what our responses produce for better or worse. This attention leads to reflection, which can further lead to questioning the assumptions that underpin the routine actions. With reflection-in-action in mind, we know it's time to experiment with trying out something different, what he calls, an "on-the-spot experiment" (1983, p. 28). In the blurred space, what arises is a more fundamental question: from where does meaningful knowledge stem? Both theory and practice are potential sources. At best, neither is privileged. Science and art are conjoined, assuming that they adhere to some methodology that finds acceptance.

This experimentation is troubling in the wide world of research and teaching, because there is no consensus and a multitude of definitions. Within the confines of traditional scientific methodology, there is a belief that agreeing upon what counts as quality investigations is possible. This assumption is never quite met, and it is the same for all methodologies. The shift to which Schön contributed, even though not deliberately, made it clearer that no research method is immune to its fuzzy context. The good news is that agreements can be made within reasonable tolerances. There is more room too for humanistic research methods that balance not only theory and practice, but as well, the need for surety and the need for knowledge that is necessary to cope with spontaneous life experiences as they unfold.

In the heat of the excitement, there was speculation in many corners, more than four, about whether the developments in research methodologies amounted to a paradigm shift—where the traditional canons were in the process of being eclipsed. Shulman (1986, 1988) thought not, and in our opinion he was right. He welcomed the plethora of methodologies that were emerging as needed, because "each of these forms of inquiry asks different questions or has different ways of asking research questions" (1988, p. 16). His focus was on the application of method, and he argued that "method is the attribute which distinguishes *research* from mere observation and speculation" (1988, p. 3). Given this attribute, this form of human discourse has room for a great deal of variety. It means that there is an order to an inquiry that sets up some kind of an objective stance, however much it is not consistent with traditional scientific canons. For the researcher, there is the possibility of choosing from an array of methods by making a personal judgment in line with his or her values. For the teacher, there is an interplay between research on teaching and the actual practice taking place. With awareness, the fuzzy world in which we live is brought into focus. The notion of being realistic is best addressed by paying attention and creatively functioning within this constraint.

Maintaining an awareness of the complexity of what affects our endeavors humanizes our work as researchers and teachers. Within a broad view that there is no method of research privileged over another, and within a broader view yet that there is no hegemony of science of any kind, methods that touch humanistic concerns are less difficult to envision. Humanistic research importantly reflects humanistic practices, practices that reflect empathy and mutually supportive human relationships. These relationships include adults with children, adults with each other, and children among themselves. The expansion of research methodologies offered choices that were commensurate with humanistic teaching practices and a framework that promised more flexibility.

RESEARCH IN FOUR WORLD VIEWS

Experimental Research

Within this same time span that qualitative research methods were developing, a six-year study was undertaken into the role of imagery in teaching and learning (Allender, 1991). Interest was sparked by a fascination with how mental imagery had been shown to facilitate problem solving, creativity, psychological and medical healing, and the more ordinary tasks that students confront in the classroom. The results of an array of previous investigations were largely positive, and this encouraged looking into the value of practical applications. In the early 1980s, Donna and Nancy Bailey expressed a readiness to involve some of their classes at Project Learn in an effort to study how mental imagery activities might be applied to subjects in their classes. Earlier research had been limited to laboratory experiments and similarly controlled studies even though they took place in the field. Unlike these investigations, the plan was to carry out the research as a part of the daily lessons. We agreed to a flexible project that would unfold from week to week, and we chose spelling, vocabulary, and arithmetic lessons because progress in students' learning is easy to quantify in all three. The plan included Jerry in the role of an assistant teacher who would help out in class on the mornings these subjects were taught.

Only a few of the insights that marked the decade at its end were yet integrated into the canons of educational research. One, though, had already gained solid ground: the need for and the respectability of introspective data—which had been ruled out by the promises of behaviorism. Here was an invitation to search the black box that represented the mind of the learner, which was deemed impenetrable for so many years. Learning theory had expanded beyond stimuli "administered" by teachers. The time had arrived to inquire into the active mental processing in which students engage. The project began with ongoing observations and conversations with students and their teachers, and led to a series of pilot studies. For these, practical problems were formulated in connection with the teaching of previous lessons. With a specific snag in mind, a concept from the imagery literature was translated into a classroom activity, and with this in hand, a lesson plan was created. Together with familiar student involvement and the characteristic independent work expected at Project Learn, the teachers engaged the students in the lesson. A log was written about what happened. On the basis of the logs of the pilot studies, the intention was to design a formal study that would approximate a standard experiment.

It seemed so simple. We were looking to construct a set of activities that involved three kinds of imagery: drawing pictures, combining images with verbal and numeral texts, and setting learning tasks within the contexts of imaginary settings, even imaginary worlds. With these, a series of lessons would be planned where comparisons could be made between the use and nonuse of imagery. We set out to document differences in test scores between using imagery or not. It was hypothesized that large differences would occur between test scores, because of the touted power of imagery. No other innovation in teaching at the time had higher expectations attached to it for making learning considerably easier. Beyond these differences, classroom discussions would probe for whether some general strategies for learning were accruing in children's minds. Successful uses of imagery as a learning tool were expected to encourage students to apply them in other situations.

However, before we got to a formal study, from the pilot studies alone, it was obvious that scores on the usual tests that students take in spelling, vocabulary, and arithmetic were not dramatically better than in previous years. To the degree that there was some improvement, it was because a child was making special progress in a particular subject. This suggested that the usefulness of the imagery tasks might be dependent on a child's specific interest. The possibility needed follow-up, but for the moment it didn't answer either of the initial questions. Furthermore, nothing observed or discussed with the children suggested that general strategies were in the making. The students were intrigued with the imagery activities and felt that they helped their learning, without considering them as unique as we supposed. Besides, whether or not using imagery in teaching and learning might have had dramatic results like those seen in laboratory tests, confusion was caused by the unusually effective learning environment that Project Learn provided without these innovations. Irrespective of the scores, the belief that the use of imagery would build an overall strategy after awhile for children's learning seemed illusory at best. The children had already built up many other personal strategies that were dependable and useful to them.

The only fair conclusion about the first year was that imagery techniques sometimes made a difference and sometimes not. Learning new vocabulary, the fundamentals of arithmetic, and to spell were greatly dependent on the styles of learning that a student already had in use, and the helpfulness of imagery was specific to particulars of the child, the lesson, and the characteristics of the imagery technique. For all this ambiguity, this was unequivocally fun teaching and learning, which counts a lot toward meeting the needs of students. The students were making good progress, even though the value of daily learning for the future was unclear. As always, at some idiosyncratic point in time, a student might begin generating a general learning strategy. The project was greatly rewarding for everyone as long as little attention was paid to the goals of the research. No one, including Jerry in his role as an assistant teacher, was fazed by the slow progress of the research.

Action Research

The teachers and students were ready to continue the work. They were pleased to learn and experience new teaching techniques. For the project, there were lingering questions to answer, and there was the obvious challenge to try a more creative methodology. First off, we let go of making comparisons. It seemed more fruitful to proceed by looking more closely at the details and the process of teaching and learning. The inquiry, now a kind of action research, was aimed at developing a greater variety and potentially more dramatic imagery activities. Together, they were the building blocks of a model teaching program. Rather than limiting the activities to those that had been found to facilitate classroom learning at ordinary schools, a larger array of imagery techniques was tapped.

A grid was constructed as a tool for suggesting the basis of these including cognitive, affective, and parapsychological dimensions. There were two main types—verbal/symbolic and visual/fantasy—and they included five kinds of learning methods for each. The use of verbal/symbolic imagery failed to achieve its purpose although it included eyes-closed hearing, eyes-closed writing, using memory aids, flagging (e.g., giving oneself an imaginary reward), and visualization. In contrast, it became clear that the process is an inroad into questioning the beliefs and assumptions that limit the ability to learn. Like boundaries that define interpersonal relationships, intrapersonal boundaries define the quality of our inner dialogue. There is much about human abilities to learn that depends on what we tell ourselves to believe and the flexibility of inner thought. The visual/fantasy ones included drawing designs, visualizing signposts (e.g., displaying a vocabulary word), drawing pictures, using special powers, and pretending magical ones. Activities were generated for the same three subjects, lesson plans were written, logs were kept, and for the next two years, the teachers and students worked together toward integrating the use of imagery into everyday teaching and learning.

An analysis of the logs created its own picture. A normality of daily lessons was established, and the students looked forward to the never-ending introduction of some new approach to learning— about one per week. The work was playful. There often were elements that made learning like playing a game, which young students almost always appreciate. And of course, there was the attraction of doing something different that was both enjoyable and relevant. There were answers to the practical questions of how to construct these activities. They did not need to be complicated or precise; just a slight shift in traditional teaching methods was enough to qualify an activity as unique. And, little insights popped up. For example, there were times when children didn't want to close their eyes when guided fantasies were involved, and it turned out that it made no difference. Children's modifications creatively added on or subtracted from some part of the instructions, and this only made the teaching and learning more interesting.

As to understanding the process better, little was accomplished. The explanations and reasons given by students either individually or in a discussion continued to be idiosyncratic. Most often, students cared little for what or why the imagery was useful to them; their attitude began to color the teachers' attitudes. The process seemed relevant only to the mind of the researcher, and this is where Jerry parted ways. It was not a bad thing, mind you. The teachers had accomplished their goals, which were very much a part of the project as a whole, and everyone was pleased with this. It was exciting teaching. But the curiosity about the process still lingered, and it was time to take a very different tack. Something about the mind, given the metaphor of the black box, resisted understanding. The use of imagery in teaching and learning worked in the sense of how it enlivened the process. Even though it didn't magically improve test scores, it clearly was a means to engaging students in their lessons.

Phenomenological Research

During the following two years, Jerry turned his attention directly to the "conversation" that occurs within the introspective mind of adults. Using the distinctly qualitative methods of phenomenology, two kinds of imagery use were explored. The first was a self-reflective inquiry into how the mind is functioning when attention is paid to imagery in the wide span of daily life activities. The second kind of imagery paralleled the learning of the Project Learn children with tasks like theirs that were heightened in difficulty so as to be a challenge for adults. For example, instead of mastering an ordinary multiplication table, the adult task was to memorize the squares from 12 to 25—a different kind of multiplication table, but an intriguing challenge. The subject of the first study was Jerry himself, and for the second, Marjorie DuBrow, Kenneth Sheinen, and Merrie Baldus, three graduate students engaged in their own mental imagery research projects took on a collaborative secondary self-study of their own thinking processes.

The solo introspection into the daily use of imagery was both frustrating and exciting. The intention to work hard on finding ways to use imagery and to analyze how they are functioning in the mind brought with it instances of strong resistance. The touted power of mental imagery came up against periods of disappointment and skepticism. Backing off from trying too hard, thus lowering the intensity of the experience, allowed for insights into the nuances of the resistance. The initial impression is that long-held learning habits stubbornly resist change, they can be modified, and imagery proved to be a useful tool for this more comprehensive purpose.

The collaborative introspections were based on an enlarged grid for generating an open-ended variety of activities. Formed by two dimensions, there were twelve cells that ranged in degree of external/internal influences on one axis and indirect/direct experience on the other. There were no limits on the number of activities that could be generated for each cell. Each of the three students worked with Jerry individually in five two-hour sessions, which were essentially in-depth interviews that took place as the learning tasks were completed. The learning methods were chosen from the grid and modified as needed. The general conclusion was that imagery is an intrinsic part of teaching and learning processes that is usually left out. When added to the mix, discussions about how learning takes place are much richer.

Much like the work with schoolchildren, the outcomes were often unexpected, yet have special value. The challenge to learn emerges as an inviting experience ahead. Movement between ordinary and fantastic uses of imagery decreases anxiety about success and increases the likelihood of noticing small successes. Some arise from the spontaneous use of mental imagery. Others are facilitated by a playfulness that detracts from the seriousness of intention. Learning is perceived to be easy. It is enhanced by constant variations, heightened contrasts, and multiple connections. The process is wholistic in the sense that students can tap a full range of strengths to find sufficient zones of comfort that ready them to take on new challenges. Their inherent curiosity and confidence generate an openness to working on what they don't know. The process is a balance between awareness and resistance that helps reduce teacher-student conflicts and release excitement for the inner restructuring of an individual's approach to learning. The focus on imagery tunes the mind into its own learning processes.

Humanistic Research

The structure of the fourth methodological world view was built into a graduate seminar entitled, "Learning About Learning with

Mental Imagery." Though not planned as a formal study, it grew into an example of humanistic research. Different than the others, which had humanistic elements, this study was an instance of what Mitroff and Kilmann (1978) had proposed as a set of methods defined by the characteristics of a particular humanist. For them, it was a theoretical idea; here, it was an instance of what until then was a null set. The methods embraced approaches to knowing that stemmed from both art and science. Personal and nonrational knowledge were counted among accepted aspects of scholarly inquiry. Unique experience was as relevant as generalizations from a body of experiences. There was room for empathy and close interpersonal relationships that developed out of collaborative conversations.

As a whole, the seminar covered the history of imagery research, its affects on cognitive and affective learning, applications to the enhancement of mental and physical abilities, and opportunities for developing personal uses of mental imagery for each student who attended the seminar. Half of the twenty-five students who enrolled were working on doctoral degrees, three were undergraduates, and the rest master's degree students. Short papers were assigned as a way of reporting on applications of imagery concepts to personal learning experiences. From the readings, students were asked to choose a concept or two that they thought could be used to improve their mental imagery skills. The assignment was to apply these skills to some aspect of daily life and to write up what happens. In all, there were 155 papers handed in over the course of the semester. Called experience/experiments, they were essentially the same format as the pilot study logs that had been collected in the previous five years.

From discussions in the large group, in small groups, and with partners who were working together on projects, it became clear early on that there was a striking similarity between Elbow's (1986) methodology of belief (versus doubt) and the need to suspend habitually held beliefs in connection with adapting imagery techniques to learning. This realization gave rise to the idea that the experience/experiments, like previous logs, were a set of data that could be analyzed as part of an organized investigation. Some of the results corroborated the findings of the third study. Focusing on imagery was rarely a superficial application of a technique. More commonly, what was involved was an in-depth personal inquiry that expanded the students' sense of what it meant to learn. And, it was equally common to experience feelings of competence— even in the face of resistance that had to be overcome. Beyond earlier findings, the discussions led to an understanding that there had to be a balance between caring and not caring about the outcome of any specific task. Overly serious pressures interrupted the ease in learning. It was better to observe what the process brings.

The broadest insights came out of a higher regard for the wisdom of practice over attention to integrated theoretical knowledge. For the most part, there were no general conditions that could be used to organize and summarize the usefulness of specific imagery techniques. The concept of a living educational theory that Jack Whitehead (1993) later proposed as a strategy for integrating personal knowledge for teachers fits the data better. The concept is enlarged by the notion that this personal knowledge is not the product of thinking that is isolated from the work of others, but rather the result of intensive collaborative conversations. Interpersonal connections place the personal theory in a kind of knowledge in community. Thus, when there were set views of seeing the world mixed with the possibilities that imagination conceived, there was a grounding in a group sense of the practical—as opposed to a loss of what is realistic. Most of the tasks set by students were quite ordinary, and still there was room for belief at times in the power of mind over matter.

DONNA, THE RESEARCHER

Two decades before there were inklings of humanistic research, we undertook the task of writing classroom materials for a study of teaching inquiry skills to elementary schoolchildren. The design of the research abided by the accepted traditional canons, but these methods did not apply to the writing of the teaching materials. Nothing about the teaching was meant to lead to correct answers. The materials were meant to encourage students to work with problems, questions, and resources aimed at engaging them in thoughtful deliberation. The goal of the research was to measure the different ways children do this kind of open-ended learning. Donna agreed to take on the major responsibility for the writing—and ended up additionally contributing most of the intuition needed to keep the teaching materials consistent with our humanistic concerns. Since that time, our continued work together as researchers has especially enhanced our collaborative conversations.

Dylan from an early age had models of teachers in his life—starting out with classes in music, art, movement, and swimming—but little in his experience suggested what a researcher does. In this letter, we wanted him to know something about Donna as a researcher. It is an introduction to another side of his grandmother that we thought he should know. The inquiry materials she wrote, *I Am the Mayor* (Allender and Allender, 1971), are described, and there is a short explanation about how they were used in the research.

Dear Dylan,

It's time to tell you something about Nana that she probably has never mentioned. You already know that she loves teaching. What you don't know is that she also likes to do research on teaching. We have worked on many projects together. And in recent years, she has taken on some of her own to present at education meetings, especially one that meets every two years in England, because it is held in a castle. For now, I'll tell you about her first big project. Another time, she can tell you about the castle.

A large orange file box on the lower shelf of the bookcase in Nana's study is the place to begin. Maybe you have noticed it. On the top it says, "I Am the Mayor." It's about a small town that she made up for children to learn social studies in a fun way. When you open the box, you'll find thirty-six file folders inside. The first two are an introduction and an example of how a student can play the role of a mayor of this town named Tinker, Colorado.

There are ten letters in the third file. Actually, there are two phone messages, two memos, a copy of the Tinker Times, *and five letters. The* Tinker Times *is not very big, but then, neither is the town—population, 12,000. The student is supposed to put them in an in-box on his or her desk. If you were playing the mayor, your job would be to read what's in the in-box and think about problems that might need to be solved. Then, you have to decide what should be done to deal with these problems.*

For example, there is a letter from the head of the Tinker Business Club asking the mayor to support the building of a new parking lot. In the right-hand margin of the letter, like there are on every page in the file box—nearly 400 of them—there are numbers across from every sentence. These page numbers lead to other files. For each letter, they lead to questions that you might want to ask.

Number 322 appears after this sentence in a letter: "If there were more parking spaces open during the shopping hours, people from towns around Tinker would be more interested in coming to Tinker to shop." Turn to page 322, and you'll find three questions. One is about how many lots there are now, the second about the number of parking spaces available, and another about other letters of concern. Each of these questions has a file number in the margin that leads to useful information. Also, there are directions for finding the index to all of the files, in case the student has some other questions in mind.

Most of the files are about Tinker—twenty in all. The questions on page 322 lead to three of these files: Town Maps, City Growth Charts, and City Letters. If you look at the index, you'll see Calendars, History, Laws, and Bulletins. Seven more files are for the Electric, Fire, Garbage and Sanitation, Park, Police, Street, and Water Departments. Then, there are Current Business files like the one for City Growth Charts. The last two files are for the mayor's letters and the city letters.

At the end of every letter, and everything else in the in-box, there is a number that leads to help on making decisions. The student mayor might decide to do nothing right now, find out something that is not in the files, or take action. Many different actions are listed from which to choose, and a student can also offer other original ideas.

For the research, there was an adult whose job it was to find the pages that a student wants to see. The adult was introduced as the mayor's secretary. Students sat at regular desks, but we put a study carrel on top. It was made of heavy cardboard covered with brown paper that looked like wood paneling, and it had three sides so it stood on the desk and felt a little bit like an office. There was a picture of Tinker and the State of Colorado seal on the side walls and a little rack near the back wall to hold the student's name card—with "The Mayor" printed below. And, there was a wooden in-box.

Dials at the bottom of the back wall were used to let the secretary—who was sitting on the other side of the carrel—know the number of the page wanted. A slot was cut underneath the dials so that pages could be passed through. There was also a pretend intercom, but really you could talk back and forth in a regular voice. The main job of the secretary was to find the correct pages and take them back when they were no longer needed. Other jobs were to help the student if need be and to talk about the work at the end of each day. For this conversation, she would come around to the office. Children only had 45 minutes each time they played the mayor, but they could come back as often as they needed to finish. Some came two times, most others worked three or four times. A few came even more times. Nearly every student enjoyed this work. If they hadn't finished, they hardly needed to be reminded. One boy wanted most of all for us to know that he really liked being mayor.

"I Am the Mayor" was written entirely so that a fourth-grader could read the information with little or no help from a teacher. Best of all, Nana wrote the whole "book" so that it is never clear whether the mayor is a boy or a girl. There were no "hims" or "hers" all the way through. Everyone who plays the mayor can pretend he or she is really in charge right now.

*Years later, when Nana was teaching at Project Learn she in-
cluded the mayor in the teaching of social studies. The nifty carrels
were long gone, and there were no secretaries in her class to help
out. But it was easy for her to have children work in pairs taking
turns being the secretary. No longer thinking about the research,
when her students finished, they got together as a class for some really good discussions. The students were intrigued by their different
approaches to dealing with the same problems. There sometimes
were as many solutions as there were students.*

*At the time, there were still enough file boxes that weren't too
worn out to use. The big problem was keeping them in order. The
bigger problem was that back when we were doing the research, no
schoolbook publisher could conceive of the usefulness of "I Am the
Mayor." We were lucky that Daniel Elazar, a friend of ours who was
the head of a special center for political science, decided to print 100
copies. Really, the kinds of computers we have today were needed.
But we didn't have them back then. When you've got some time, ask
Nana to play "I Am the Mayor" with you.*

Love, Grangran

HEGEMONY OR PARTNERSHIP?

Humanistic educational research is rooted in well-established relationships between teachers and researchers. The purpose is to
ensure that the process and outcomes of scholarly inquiry have a
good chance of being applicable to practical problems—the ones
that the people who work directly with children have to face daily
in their schools and classrooms. Historically, investigators were
not concerned with how teachers related to the results of their research. This has changed in recent years, in effect bringing the
needs of the two closer. The gap between them has grown considerably smaller as academic faculty and teachers have learned to
work together cooperatively. There is now widespread recognition
that educational research is likely to be meaningless without attention to the dynamics of everyday practical problems.

Ironically, the gap, though smaller, also has ways of being unwittingly maintained by the well-intended interactions of teachers
and researchers. The pressures in the classroom typically make it
difficult to find time for thinking through the complex dynamics
that contribute to everyday problems. When disruptions occur,
they usually require immediate amelioration, leaving the underlying larger scope of dissatisfactions—of students, the teacher, or
both—unaddressed. On the other side, doing research is time con-

suming and often frustrating. The pressures are unlike the immediacy of classroom problems, but they are equally real. Top most among the pressures are the demands created by the desire to do quality research. What value can an inquiry have without meeting this standard? For all the careful efforts, there is frustration around every corner. As a consequence, the practitioners and investigators both want quick fixes to make classroom life easier, with high priorities placed on developing new tricks for handling troublesome moments.

Results like these, however, are unlikely to be applicable without attention to the specific dynamics of each unique classroom. The gap reappears and contributes to a lack of commitment on the part of teachers to make an effort to see applicability. The problem is affected by the a priori belief that academic inquiry is not practical. There are times, too, where studies become policy and are used to mandate how teachers should teach and test, and this is sure to interfere with collaboration. More likely, used in this way, research will create resistance to taking new ideas seriously. In reality, theoretical efforts even when backed by empirical investigations are not going to be viewed as having anything to do with the children sitting in a teacher's classroom. Sadly, teachers are then accused of not being interested in improving.

It would seem that an awareness of these conflicts would be enough to correct the discordant views. What we've learned is that the discord is systemic and sometimes borders on intractable. Our working together as both researchers and teachers has bridged the gap that many others feel on both sides, but not without difficult conflicts that needed to be worked out. Our way out has been to assume that it is more a matter of confronting the conflicts rather than resolving them—finding comfortable compromises, and not absolute solutions. We began by depending on the addition of qualitative research methods to the canon. Their lack of rigidity provided greater space for negotiating our principally different responsibilities, while broadening our understanding of the implications and potential applications of the research. The process began with valuing each other's needs and believing that educational research is most valuable when it is undertaken as a cooperative adventure helping children to learn.

The belief that educational research trumps practice, historically and still, is one of the major obstacles. The results of scholarly inquiry have managed to become the top of a top-down world. The not-so-subtle message is that there is a better known way to teach, and teachers ought to change their practices accordingly. And, teachers have a way of willingly participating in this system when they persist in searching for the new trick to quickly and magically make their teaching easier. Progress depends on giving up the hegemony of scholarly inquiry. Knowledge has many sources, and they are best honored when they are used as part of a lively dialectic. The obvious shift for an academic is to give credit to teachers for the practical knowledge they have acquired from experience. In so many ways, there is no truer knowledge. The less obvious shift is for teachers to give themselves credit for having an expertise that is uniquely valuable to themselves, and others too.

Somewhere in history, the status of the teaching profession lost ground—setting up teachers to be viewed as incompetent. This view handicaps every teacher, and there is a dire need to escape this undeserved status. We can work on changing social systems. But, waiting around is detrimental; one has to begin with bringing together evidence of self-worth. There are always some successes that can be remembered, just as self-worth is boosted by positive feedback even though there has been very little of it. This start, taken together with finding a bit of time to explore what is going on in the classroom in a more nuanced way, has a chance of initiating change that makes a difference. With a less immediate need to confront a sense of inferiority, there is a higher degree of motivation to engage more fully. Under these conditions, knowledge from other sources is more appealing. What is required for cooperative work is give and take on all sides, but we have to work with what we have. We aim toward valuing each other's needs, knowing that educational research is most valuable when there is mutual support.

Responding to a challenge for change not only serves children, it enlivens teachers. Doing the same thing year after year without looking reflectively at what one is doing is tiring and leads to early retirement. Taking time to think with another person about what one is doing and how it serves inner needs as well as students' needs stimulates possibilities and ideas. There isn't a teacher in a classroom who does not have a problem that is nagging her or him about what is happening every day. With a climate that encourages reflection, discussion, and experimentation, teachers become experts not just in their subjects, but as well in recognizing the needs of students. There is little doubt that every teacher really wants a lively, engaging classroom that meets the needs of every child who enters the room. Though ideals are rarely achieved, the teacher who garners knowledge from different perspectives, and differing visions, is sure to be enlivened. As a model, a message gets to the students that cooperation and change are possible.

8

The Self-Study of Teaching Teachers

A small notice in the *Educational Researcher*, the flagship journal of the American Educational Research Association (AERA), with the help of some word of mouth brought together a group of over 200 members at the 1993 annual meeting—to explore the value of studying their own practices as teacher educators. In essence, as a part of a newly formed special interest group within the auspices of the parent organization, they asked themselves whether the manner of their teaching was consistent with how they taught teachers to teach. So ready were they for a group like this, calling themselves the Self-Study of Teacher Education Practices, their research was in high gear almost from the first moments of its formation.

THE VISION OF THE SELF-STUDY COMMUNITY

The International Handbook of Self-Study of Teaching and Teacher Education Practices (Loughran, Hamilton, LaBoskey, and Russell, 2004) chronicled the history of the special interest group during its first decade. The publication of the handbook was a major event in the establishment of the field of self-study research. As one of the contributors, Jerry discussed the overarching humanistic elements and influences that were integral to this kind of research (Allender, 2004). Five years earlier in the *Educational Researcher*, Ken Zeichner (1999) had already marked its potential as one of the new forms of scholarship. Typical of any humanistic endeavors in education, the attention paid to self-study by most of the members of AERA, upward of 20,000 and growing, was relatively small. Yet, there was an abundance of conversation motivated by worries that crediting self-study as a methodology would undermine the trustworthiness of educational research. This suggested more interest than admitted. Some of the methods did deviate at times from the norms and appeared to threaten accepted canons. In a positive light, the character of the self-study research early on was proving itself to be distinct from other means of investigation (Hamilton, 1998). It was this shift that was intriguing.

Self-study is, of course, not new. Widespread cultural values embrace the belief that an unexamined life is not worth living. Though sometimes offered up as a platitude, this is a truth that pervades educated human experience. The relevance of the field of psychotherapy attests to the ubiquitous recognition of its importance. For teachers, there have always been autobiographies, often distinguished and popular, that fill this role for both the writer, and the reader vicariously. Wonderful examples over the past five decades include *Summerhill* (Neill, 1960), *Teacher* (Ashton-Warner, 1963), *P.S. Your [sic] Not Listening* (Craig, 1972), *Growing Minds* (Kohl, 1984), *We Make the Road by Walking* (Horten and Freire, 1990), and *Teacher Man* (McCourt, 2005). Whenever teachers talk or write about their teaching, it is an opportunity for self-study. What is unique in the AERA self-study community is that there are teacher educators who have dedicated their work to self-understanding. There are too many times when we as academics belie our education curriculum by not practicing what we are preaching. The Self-Study of Teacher Education Practices community was foremost founded to actively confront this contradiction.

On the surface, this academic self-study appeared to be just another innovation that fit with the developments of qualitative research that began in the 1980s. The methods were borrowed in their entirety from those that had been in use for many years. There were many variations of action research, most of which were aimed at collecting field data and using it to inform the improvement of ongoing programs. Other studies depended on the methods of narrative inquiry and autoethnography. The stories told became the foundation of expanded reflective teaching. And, not infrequently, an arts-based approach to research broadened understanding with insightful performances, the visual arts, and sometimes dance and music. The application of quantitative methods was not out of the question, but the use of the more creative forms of research was more productive. The central purposes of self-study were best accommodated by the opportunities and possibilities that qualitative methods offered.

Surprisingly, a pattern of studies emerged following two separate paths. In one direction, probing one's own teacher education practices honed in on questions about specific classroom practices. What were the methods of teaching? Were the results in line with expected achievement? How could this teaching be done better? The other path was an inquiry into the nature and role of the teacher self. What are existing strengths? What interpersonal skills need development? How does vulnerability fit into the picture? Initially, there were conflicts in the community over this difference. Some placed the second as more serious and worthy than the first. Aiming directly toward finding the best practices was more likely to meet the standards of quality scholarship. Over the years, in a spirit of collaboration, a space for all manner of self-studies was seen as an inclusive and honest strategy for integrating the field into the mainstream (Loughran and Russell, 2002; Tidwell and Fitzgerald, 2006). The obvious became more obvious in recognizing the striking differences between teachers.

Tension between the canonical methods and personal differences complicates the research. Ordinarily, methodological standards are set for every kind of research. These standards (even if they are broadly defined when qualitative methods are in use) take precedence because they insure the possibility of applying the results to other situations. Problematically, the first and foremost objective of self-study is a search for personal knowledge. Having this objective and acting on it is what places the research within the definition of an authentic self-study. To achieve both is not impossible, but often, the rules are bent in the direction of privileging self-knowledge. It is the power of self-knowledge obtained through a personal search with the assistance of challenging collaborators that is in the foreground. Compromises that are necessarily made press on the requirements of the research methods in service of the needs of the self. The self is given a slight edge. This is the distinction, though controversial, that self-study carries.

For teachers the goal of self-study is to come closer to fulfilling ideals—by closing a gap between an educational vision and what is practiced in the classroom. Jack Whitehead (1993) formulated it as a "living contradiction" that is always in search of resolution. He further offers the concept of a "living theory" that is formulated by a teacher out of data that arises from self-study. The hundreds of self-studies that have already been carried out by members of the community (cf. Loughran et al., 2004) were done with the hope of improving their own teaching and influencing other teacher educators and classroom teachers as well. Even with less surety than is accomplished by other kinds of research, all studies serve as models to clarify the path ahead. But because the gap will never be closed completely, the process of making it narrower is never ending. As circumstances are bound to bring new difficulties, the gap will widen again. Visions are ephemeral, yet hopeful. And, hope is strength.

All teachers can inch toward narrowing the distance between their ideals and their practice when they rise above daily struggles. The struggles have at their root an insufficient understanding of the power of self-knowledge—complicated by the fear of a possible loss of integrity and the likelihood of being a poor role model for students and other teachers. Personal visions become compromised, thus the gap. Without vibrant visions, professors of education in particular cannot expect that new and veteran teachers will manage to keep theirs in place. Where lies the fault? It's easy to see a myriad of causes. Everyone in the system contributes to the problem, from the teachers and students themselves, the administrators, the parents, the policymakers, to everyone else who acts like a stakeholder.

For all that educational research has been transformed by humanistic concerns, it does not include the birth and care of personal vision. Long-standing tradition places the high prospects of what education is meant to achieve within the domain of philosophy; the high standards of research methodology are intended to ensure that the knowledge acquired to realize the philosophical goals is sound. The assumptions are based on idealistic and practical considerations, but in either case, though many restrictive traditions were undone in the more recent transformations of research methods, the separation of evidence and value still has been maintained. It is recognized that quality research is substantially influenced by context. It is no longer believed that an investigator can be disinterested in the process of establishing knowledge—as was the norm for much of the twentieth century. Yet, though there is a tacit hold to the notion that research is value laden, it should not be value driven.

We know that acquiring knowledge is influenced by personal needs. To change the accepted standards for the ways knowledge is acquired may seem counterintuitive. The privileged goal of research is to convey knowledge that has general application. The privileged position of educational research, by virtue of its status, interferes with the self-knowledge required by classroom teachers to interact successfully with students in the ongoing immediate moments of teaching. The needed strength of personal confidence vies with imagining that there are more accurate solutions to problems that lie outside of oneself. In our minds, the value of surety is balanced by knowing that the self-study research always serves as a model for others. This is not to say that there is little else to learn from teacher educators, but for practical reasons alone, it serves teachers to privilege the whole of the knowledge they have learned from all sources, particularly as it is assimilated into personal knowledge. From this position, teachers at all levels can act with integrity and behave as role models for their students in ways that demonstrate personal growth, learning, and enthusiasm for the jobs to be done.

DONNA'S POSTCARDS FROM THE HERSTMONCEUX CASTLE

Every other year since 1996, about 100 educators who are members of the Self-Study Special Interest Group, professors in the main and others including some classroom teachers, have been gathering at the Herstmonceux Castle in England to share their current research. Typically, midsummer over a five-day period, three or four one-hour concurrent sessions are scheduled and normally divided in two for a presentation and an interactive discussion. The formal papers are published and distributed to the conferees at the beginning of the conference to facilitate dialogue. Many of the publications that are cited in this chapter were outgrowths of these proceedings. It's an exciting conference that is supportive and challenging.

Dear Dylan,

Grangran and I are in England at the Herstmonceux Castle in East Sussex. We are here for a conference with educators who come every two years from all over the world to work together on making schools better for children. This year there are friends from the United States, England, Canada, Australia, New Zealand, Belgium, Germany, Iceland, South Africa, and the Netherlands.

It really is fun to spend five days of meetings in an old English castle, which has turrets and crenels all around the top. We were told that the original lord had to pay the king a tax for each one of the crenels. One room has a trapdoor leading down to a dungeon. The meals are served in a grand hall. It might be fun to sleep in the castle, but alas there is a comfortable dormitory for the people attending conferences. It looks just like a castle you would draw. There's a moat too, but sad to say, it doesn't go all around the way anymore. In recent years, someone blocked it off to build a garden in the back, which actually is a beautiful place to sit or stroll. Frankly, I wish the moat still went full circle. Don't you?

Love, Nana

Dear Dylan,

Today, I went to a session presented by Robyn Brandenburg from Australia. She spoke about how she changed her teacher education classes from just lecturing to having discussions with her students. She was pleased with the change but was curious about how to set up the discussions so that everyone in class would participate. The research explored her concerns about those students who do not talk in class and what is therefore left unsaid. There was a very lively discussion and some real disagreement. Some folks thought it was the right of the students not to talk and others felt it was their obligation to contribute their thinking to the group. Interestingly, there were people in the session who didn't talk at all but that was not explored. When this session was over, my friend Sandy Schuck from Australia and I continued the debate during the morning teatime and several people gathered around to listen and add their thoughts about silent students. We had trouble stopping so we could get to the next session on time. It is fun to be with lively people.

Love, Nana

Dear Dylan,

I gave my presentation this morning. I'm so glad it's over. It was good enough, but the topic and the problem still bother me. It's true that doing this study was fun. I had asked all the junior high students at PL to answer two questions about their own and their teachers' responsibility for learning. I also asked all the teachers and some of the kids' parents. It is worrisome, though, to realize how difficult it is for folks to understand that responsibility for learning belongs most of all to the students, even in a school where this clearly is the assumption. Students appreciate humanistic education, yet want their teachers to give them answers and tell them exactly what to do. There was a good discussion of these concerns, but my confusion lingers. How can we help students to accept their responsibility for learning?

Love, Nana

Dear Dylan,

One of my special friends is Stefinee Pinnegar from Utah. We make a point of spending time talking whenever we are together at a meeting. This afternoon, we sat for an hour on a bench in the inner courtyard of the castle talking about what was important to us in our work and some changes we need to make. It's been a beautiful, sunny day and other people at the conference were there too but somehow had the sense to leave the two of us alone. I know you have special friends, so you can understand how I feel.

Last night, Stefinee brought hundreds of different construction materials to the pub. The pub is a modern addition, but it feels ancient there in a corner of the castle that once served as the guardhouse. It opens to the bridge over the moat. Anyway, she taught us how to make little dolls similar to the ones folks make in Guatemala. We had such a good time, and we laughed so much. The dolls were all attached to a hat made for Tom Russell who had the idea for having the conference and organized it. It was Stefinee's way for all of us to thank Tom while having a really good time together and getting to know each other in a playful and creative way.

Love, Nana

JERRY'S TEACHER SELF

In the early 1990s, a year or two before the self-study group was formed, I formed an idea for a narrative study of my teaching. Partly, the thinking was influenced by a small group of professors under the leadership of Fred Lighthall (a former teacher and subsequent colleague from the University of Chicago) that met to discuss our research from a personal point of view. Plus, I wanted to try a hand at writing stories as an inroad to a better understanding of the teaching and learning process, my own in particular. The project was in full bloom at the advent of the new self-study special interest group. I assigned the writing of a story to my students as the culminating evaluation for the Art and Science of Teaching and began writing my stories as well. Some of them were joined together into a book, entitled, *Teacher Self: The Practice of Humanistic Education* (2001). The result was a reflection and meditation on what was going on in classes, over the period of a semester, from both the students' point of view and my own.

Nearing retirement, the idea for the narrative study had surfaced in response to feelings about teaching this undergraduate course, under a variety of names, for more than thirty years. I felt stuck. I knew that it would be possible to slide through teaching at this point in my career, but the collaboration with Fred Lighthall and continued interest in research required more—in addition to my inner sense of wanting to bring my ideals and practices closer together. The teaching was good enough, but with only a little more reflection, I realized that I was stuck in an okay groove. Not my style. There were no serious problems demanding resolution, but there was resistance to change. I blamed the administration, lack of cooperation from colleagues, disinterested students, you name it, all this for my willingness to do just a "good enough" job. Discussions with Donna made it easy to see that I was giving in to a loss of power. Moving ahead with the project, pushing aside fears that were mostly groundless, and writing lesson plans aimed at having a better chance of getting good stories were all rewarding. I felt closer to my earlier years as a teacher, when enthusiasm and sincerity carried me through difficult classes. As the project moved along, I gained more insights into generating successful plans, the flexibility that responded better to students' needs, and how a sense of confidence can be renewed. My teacher self benefited wholly from the work. The students' work and reactions affirmed the value. Most of the struggle involved agonizing over the writing. There were teaching glitches, but certainly no more than before. Probably less, because there was a higher level of ease.

The interwoven stories in *Teacher Self* covered a range of issues. They were all important to me, though some seemed of more serious concern than others. Lighter at least on the surface were the ones that dealt with temporary discomforts caused by unfamiliar experience as opposed to those connected with confrontation growing out of interpersonal tensions. It was mostly fun during the first week of class when the students and I learned each other's names. The lesson was used to exemplify the idiosyncratic nature of learning and how different approaches function—with an emphasis on the usefulness of mental imagery. And, assignments that mixed conceptual thinking with the production of art were enticing, even when they were initially off-putting. More problematic, however, were the times when bad feelings were involved. Because of my regular attempts to maximize choice for everyone in class, usually a good thing, a student once found himself humiliated when no one would choose to be in a group he volunteered to lead. Writing this story forced me to recognize the levels of responsibility that teachers have for guiding the formation of groups—for both children and adults. In another lesson, the problem of memorizing multiplication tables was addressed by asking adult students to learn the squares of 12 to 25. A math major touched upon his arrogance when he assumed that he didn't have to do the work. Consequently, he failed the test that others in class with much less expertise passed easily. His comeuppance painfully taught him an important lesson and alerted me to some of my own entitlement.

The stories in every case enlightened my teacher self, and the students who served as coauthors attributed similar reactions to their growth. For me, a better grasp of how to match my ideals and practices emerged. It is a special accomplishment when the teacher and the students in a teacher education class are able to share a common goal for the development of their teacher selves.

Especially intriguing is how sometimes there is little difference in the process for novices and experts.

Midway through the semester, the students were assigned to write a typical midterm paper. Donna predictably insisted that I write one too—ending up as a chapter in *Teacher Self* (2001) that separated the fifth story from the last four. After some heartfelt procrastination, as in, "this assignment does not really apply to me" (not unlike the thoughts and behavior of some of the students), I finally alighted on a topic: the problem of realness. As we discussed in Chapter 2, Rogers (1969) guided the basic tenets of my teaching with three major concepts. The first, treating students with acceptance, had always been the easiest to apply. There is always something about a student's work, usually a lot, that can be appreciated and even prized. Expressing these sentiments is not a skill that is so difficult to develop. It requires only attention to its importance and a bit of creativity. The second, empathic understanding, is a little more difficult. Yet, valuing and engaging in unusually careful listening is likely to engage this source of emotion. Without minimizing the ambiguity involved, and the possible mistakes that can be made, empathy is a skill for which practice helps. Realness is the trickiest of the three. Knowledge about realness is often derived from a negative message. It's an internal message, gathered from thoughts, feelings, and even physical sensations, that is triggered when the teacher self (or any other aspect of our self, for that matter) is being seriously compromised. Serious? How does one know? Compromise is a part of life. The issue is one of integrity, and there is no steady standard.

There is a complex interaction among our senses of vulnerability, tendencies toward resistance, efforts to build mutually supportive relationships, and the generative relevance of excitement. Adding the last idea to the mix was the fresh idea that came to mind as a result of writing the midterm. Excitement for teaching is what is involved in being interested, engaged, lively, hopeful, and everything else that a person associates with what makes life worth living. Resistance protects us, vulnerability opens us to the unknown, attention to relationship is what we're aiming for, and excitement for the job is what we get when the mix is on target. A healthy teacher self does not exist as an unchanging entity; developing the self is a process that responds to internal growth and the ups and downs that the classroom environment readily provides. It is the opposite of stuck. When a person's actions take these factors into account, an authenticity is experienced that I call *realness*. As I began, realness is tricky and highly desirable. Finishing the paper, not quite on time, helped me get closer.

In the first years the teacher self develops as a person moves from the idea to choose the profession, acquires the credentials, gets through the first year, and looks forward (or not) to the experiences ahead over the years to come. There's no avoiding it; it happens. It's what Richard Lipka and Thomas Brinthaupt (1999) call "the role of self in teacher development." There is a complex weave of personal and professional traits, mixed in with attentions given to knowledge of subject matter, teaching techniques, and looking inward at growing concepts of philosophy, psychology, and strengths and weaknesses. For some, the growth is mostly about subject matter, and for others, there is more attention paid to teaching techniques. In the beginning, a strong contender for my attention was the development of confidence. And, built into the discussion of this development was a tacit hint that a well-meaning teacher will work on the development of a healthy self-concept. For the two of us, it was more about doing the job and trying to spare some time to reflect on what's happening inside. For all that reflective teaching has become a normal expectation, awareness is a precious commodity that is often hard to come by. The problem worsens when uncomfortable or more difficult feelings are released by this awareness.

The time needed to do the work leading to greater understanding and the development of the teacher self is usually difficult to find. There are many pressures from our daily personal and professional lives that compete. For teacher educators who do manage to find time for research, the reflection and research become one and the same. There are some classroom teachers among us, like Donna, who manage at a greater expense. But typically, the priority for work that expands one's awareness rises to the top only when seemingly insurmountable problems are being encountered. Whatever the conditions, clearly it takes creative management of the other priorities to find the time. Most teachers understand that the awareness created by self-study expands possibilities and provides better preparation to meet students' needs and their own. Especially in the face of difficult conditions, keeping ourselves lively and successful depends on not being discouraged. No really good advice applies in general. With or without helpful collaboration, a personal store of creative energy is all we have.

FINDING POWER IN PRACTICE

Recently, in an essay on the practical and scholarly value of our work, Jerry concluded, "The future holds the possibility that every educator will assume at times an attitude of self-study, whether as a reflective teacher or towards undertaking a rigorous investigation" (Allender, 2005, p. 104). The essay was one of fifteen that were included in a book that addressed the question, *What Difference Does Research Make and for Whom?* (Bodone, 2005). In general, concerned attention was paid to questioning the assumptions that underpin research methods, bringing to the surface unrecognized sources of voice, and concretizing how local action leads to global impact. As a whole, there is obviously more to any body of meaningful research than a figural focus on self, but then again it is only on the body of individual selves that application can depend. What became clear is how all research has the potential for enlightening practitioners, but not principally because of the expertise it bequeaths. Traditionally, there is a one-to-one relationship between the quality of research and the trust that is warranted. Thus, irrespective of self-knowledge, it is held that the knowledge obtained through research is more valuable than any other. By challenging this assumption, there is room to shape an attitude of self-study so that it supports a sense of agency—integrating knowledge from many sources. With this view, scholarly research is only part of a process that productively strengthens voice, hones a sense of individual and local agency, and, by joining with others, increases the likelihood of larger impacts, which can sometimes be global.

Closest to home, the place to study and learn about oneself is by doing the same work that is required of students and experiencing what they experience. When the learning is on an adult level, simply doing the same tasks and tests is on target; sometimes, what is required are similar tasks that have been adapted to a more appropriate level of difficulty. For example, when a teacher writes a research paper that is required of the students, there is a better chance of feeling empathy and grasping students' problems of learning more intuitively. Maybe a platitude, but indeed nothing else sets up a better mirror than putting oneself in another's shoes. In Rogers's (1969) terms, now applied to the "student," realness is unavoidable as the teacher goes about doing a task similar to the one set for others. The need to do well is paramount as is wanting to be appreciated for effort and accomplishments. For sure, these factors might not be important in situations where being the student is no more than giving simple answers to questions on a test. However, when teacher educators go back to elementary or high school classrooms to face the normal expectations put upon student teachers, there is not enough expertise around to insure all will go smoothly. Unforeseen events make teaching a challenge for novice or expert. Needing empathy, struggling with realness, and depending on acceptance are given conditions, making the trio of the Rogerian concepts complete and understandable.

Professors in the Classroom

Stefinee Pinnegar (1995), so long a college professor, wondered whether her competence to again be a student teacher, like the ones she was supervising, might have greatly diminished over the years. She took up the challenge. Her placement was not unlike any other that was assigned to the students, except that a former student who was supportive of her plan and now the lead teacher in an eighth grade public school made the arrangements. But the teacher who would be her supervisor was skeptical that a college professor could be any more competent than the novices who were regularly assigned. Because of this skepticism, Stefinee was entrusted with no more responsibilities than they, which essentially was a constraint on her personal strengths as a teacher. To capture the experience, she wrote daily reflections and added clarifications and expansions later when she transcribed the notes into a more readable form. She found herself in the position of needing to build her supervisor's as well as the students' trust, and upon reflection, realized the multiple levels with which she, like her students, must constantly cope.

Turning her past knowledge upside down, Pinnegar (1995) had to go "beyond the question of whether theories, ideas, and research taught in teacher education programs are evident in the practice of teachers . . . to focus instead on *how such learning is evident*" (p. 67, italics in the original). Doing so suggested that problems of practice were better handled by observing the ways in which theories and ideas emerge in her students, and herself. These observations offered a cogent insight into how teaching skills develop.

Using another approach, Tom Russell (1995) partnered with a high school physics teacher. Tom taught one of his high school physics classes, and the partner taught one section of Tom's physics educational methods course at the university. Action research methods, with a more formal design than the Pinnegar study, guided the collection of data. The project began with the formulation of questions about his practices, how they might be improved, and the kinds of evidence needed to insure the validity of the results. The sources of data included discussions with his partner, college students, and high school students as well as their observations of him. Formulating the meaning of the data, Tom described the tensions among reason, position, and experience. Self-study is mainly about learning from experience and privileging this knowledge. Yet, these other factors—reason and position—detracted from this viewpoint. Overriding tradition, he noticed that all of them could contribute to the whole. He recognized the importance of more experienced support, mirroring Pinnegar's lack thereof, and academic knowledge, while struggling to keep self-knowledge intact. He was "struck by the eternal gap between coursework at Queen's [University] and practice in schools" (p. 108) and appreciated how physics methods students were willing to push on him with productive criticism and even back talk, something he prized. He came to understand how "voice is a vehicle for reflective practice" (quoting from Richert, 1992, p. 192), seeing how his voice had grown along with his students'.

In the same vein, John Loughran and Jeff Northfield (1996) undertook a yet more complex study that touched on unsolvable difficulties. They were two university professors who took on the job together: one went back to teach in a junior high school and the other came along to observe and keep a log. They were joined by a graduate student who interviewed some of the students. With the added complexity, they were able to explore many problems and nuances that are involved in the process, and Jeff Northfield, the teacher in this study, was often disappointed. His conclusions reflected the discomfort of embracing the conflicting knowledge of what should be done and what could be done—intractable problems that all teachers encounter. Though more realistic than pessimistic, these conclusions face us with how difficult are the problems teachers face and how palpable the discomforts of self-study can be.

Self-Study Research Methods

There are many other varieties of self-study. They differ widely in purpose, method, and design. A few examples should suffice to demonstrate the breadth of possibilities for both educational researchers and classroom teachers. Autobiographical studies are among the most prevalent and important. They have been used to mine a teacher's history as a student, young or old, and the experience of becoming a teacher or finally, a teacher of teachers. Some of these are not unlike the letters we have written to Dylan. The overall breadth includes an expansion of the concept of research tools, the introduction of visual techniques, and the adaptation of artistic performance to the habits and requisites of scholarly inquiry. Deborah Tidwell and Linda Fitzgerald (2006) found a range that varied along the lines of autobiography, theory, classroom practices, collaboration, and modes of representing research. Nor was the gamut meant to limit possibilities; it is better thought of as a heuristic for finding a design that best suits a teacher's curiosity and commitment.

The autobiographical work of Anastasia Samaras (2002), an example from the beginning of this century, is especially intriguing. She accepted Whitehead's (1993) challenge to formulate a living theory. With less attention on his concept of living contradictions, she focused on stories of growing up in a traditional Greek family all the while interpreting her experiences through the lens of Vygotskian learning theory (cf. Vygotsky, 1978). It was in part an exploration of family, beginning before her birth, and personal history from childhood until the present. Concomitantly, the history was analyzed in terms of social and cultural influences that shaped her development, the more specific contexts of daily learning, the ways in which corresponding cognition was socially mediated, and how this education led and continues to lead her development as a teacher educator. It became clear how the stories of growing up reflected her unique needs as a student and pointed at the great importance of knowing her students' stories. The analysis brought to life an evocative sense of who she is for her benefit and the reader's—also bringing to life Vygotskian theory. Hers was a passion for ideas that integrate experience to create, in mind and heart, a deeper understanding of what learning means and how it can better be facilitated. On this basis, she had formulated a living theory that guides her teaching.

As part of expanding the concept of research tools, Mary Manke and Jerry proposed the interpretation of artifacts as a source of data collection—much the same as an anthropologist would do—in connection with a study that addresses issues of classroom diversity. From more than ten years of collaborative research on self-study methodology, they had constructed a schema that includes artifacts, reflection as a metaphor, reanalysis, narrative, collaboration, improvisation, performance, emotional and relational research, and the value of unpredictability. Here, they drew out stories attached to a collection of old classroom materials and new photographs taken to evoke self-understanding. Problems of understanding diversity issues were the target of investigation; discovering insights into personal obstacles for resolving them was the goal. Besides achieving practical insights for themselves as teachers, they enlarged an understanding of artifacts as a research tool. In conclusion, they advise,

> The term *artifacts* includes both objects remaining from the past research and objects created specifically to represent concepts in current self-studies. So look in your file drawers and your storage boxes to find

artifacts—but also consider using your own creative abilities, poetry, other writings, visual expressions of all kinds, musical and theatrical activities. . . . [T]hey become artifacts, objects . . . that can enlighten you in ways you did not expect when you first worked with them. (Manke and Allender, 2006, pp. 262–263)

Their artifacts successfully facilitated the study of diversity by their ability to become objects of reflection. The study also broadened understanding of self-study methodology.

The concept of nodal moments (Tidwell, 2006) brought together the visual representation of classroom experiences that any teacher could draw and the idea that there are significant moments worthy of analysis and interpretation that regularly occur within these experiences. The drawings are informal and might occur spontaneously as in doodles while teaching, reflectively as one contemplates recent teaching events, or retrospectively, from the rereading of entries in a weekly journal. In an effort to improve the practice of teaching, and ultimately to help others improve theirs, Deborah Tidwell collected a series of her spontaneous and reflective drawings. From an analysis, she found evidence of embodied living contradictions that signaled sites of discrepancy between intention and practice. A discussion of these instances served as a catalyst for improving her classroom teaching. She then applied the same methods to the teaching of preservice teachers to help them better understand their initial teaching experiences, and finally, found them an excellent means for creating thoughtful discussions about teaching with students and colleagues. In each case, two nodal moment questions were posed: What is happening? Why is this important? In conclusion, she proposed that finding nodal moments "provides the impetus for your reflective discussions, and provides the artifact for deconstructing a moment in time. . . . It is the discussions, questions and prompts among you and your colleagues that form the frame for your reflective practice" (Tidwell, 2006, p. 284).

One of the best contenders for finding power in practice is dramatic performance. Intellect, emotions, and the body are all involved with the addition of the excitement and anxieties that come with having an audience. Even when the script, or the structure of an improvisation, is not meant as a kind of rehearsal for teaching, the learning that takes place for the performers and the audience has a high potential of being transformative. Not an original idea, Arts-Based Educational Research, another special interest group of AERA established before self-study was founded, provided the know-how. With this support, a small number of plays appeared at the Herstmonceux Castle during the past ten years. Memorable among them were "Dance Me to an Understanding of Teaching" in 1998 and "Prom Dresses Are Us?" in 2000. In these, learning to tap dance as an adult (Cole and McIntyre, 2001) and reflecting on the meaning of a teacher's clothing (Weber and Mitchell, 2004) brought to life on stage the pain and enthusiasm that coursed with the blood of the star and costar in each play to reveal the extraordinary joy that teachers and their students can find in the classroom.

A play about shoes also comes to mind, because we have been so concerned about walking in someone else's. In 2002, Sandra Weber and Claudia Mitchell performed "When the Shoe Doesn't Fit: Death of a Salesman" on the Herstmonceux Castle's makeshift stage. In their previous play, Sandra had supported Claudia's exploration of how teachers dress. In the last moment of that performance, Sandra became aware of her own unique history that led to this new adventure: "As I stood there holding a shoe in my hand (as demanded by the script)—click—I realized all at once how important shoes could be as a method of inquiry into my teaching, how shoes could force me to confront things I was ignoring by other methods of self-study. Shoes would make me confront and reconsider my past. Thus began a series of self-studies using shoes" (Weber, 2005, p. 16). The truth of it began with a father who had been a serious shoe salesman with ideals about quality—in a quest for success. And after his death, a relative commented on how her father's job was similar to Sandra's. Getting beyond the thought of an insult, Sandra asked, "Me—a salesman?" "Yes—she replied—But instead of loving, designing, and selling shoes, you love, design and peddle ideas" (p. 19).

"The aim of self-study research is to provoke, challenge, and illuminate rather than confirm and settle." These are the words of Robert Bullough and Stefinee Pinnegar (2001, p. 20) from their discussion of how quality research is achieved. Sandra and Claudia could have had no other goals in mind when they performed their plays at the castle in 2000 and 2004. We still must question, though, in what way can these performances be counted as research? There is a relationship between the borrowed methods of more traditional research and the creative forms of inquiry that are used in self-studies. As Bullough and Pinnegar discuss, they create a balance that avoids telling more personal stories than are needed while maintaining an effort to achieve the professional goals that have been set. It is a balance that humanizes the canon. The authority of the investigation is established in two ways: partially framing a study within research traditions and succeeding in convincing oneself and others that the study has proven worthwhile. Usually, good enough writing is required, because this is how experience is transformed into story. It is the story that becomes the object of reflection, not the experience, because in its "untruth," a fruitful realness is created. Then, this object of reflection brings with it a kind of objectivity that is qualitatively different than simple reactions to experience, "mere opinion" as it is often said. The object of reflection is essentially what Allan Feldman (2003) argues is the source of validity for a self-study. In the final analysis, dramatic representation in self-study is not just entertaining but necessary to accomplish its unique goals.

Standard criticism likens our work to navel gazing and other such intended epithets. The wide range of methods available for the study of the teacher self makes it possible for classroom teachers to engage in this process without undue difficulty; the hegemonic force of the traditional canon is offset as every researcher and teacher is invited to participate. Self-study is not an exclusive club. Any interested educator can develop expertise, and the work is sure to develop some new powers for the practice of teaching. "Failing to grasp that looking inward can lead to a more intelligent and useful *outward gaze* is to seriously misunderstand the method and potential of narrative and autobiographical forms of inquiry" (Mitchell and Weber, 2005, p. 4). Self-study is for all practical purposes coterminous with finding power in practice.

9

Global Impact

Looking back over the past fifty years, our contribution to the humanistic changes in education that have occurred gives us a sense of accomplishment. Wondering about the value of our efforts started us on the writing of this book; working together with young students, their parents, teacher education students, teachers, administrators, and our academic colleagues has enriched our lives and made it possible. It may seem far-fetched to believe that concern for humanistic education is alive and well; though often hidden in the shadows and rarely the dominant mode of thinking, it still regularly finds its way into school practices worldwide.

THE EVIDENCE

In our thinking, there are two kinds of accomplishment. There are the more obvious changes that usually do not stir up a sense that they are the result of radical influences. They are taken as a norm for modern (or postmodern if you will) teacher behavior and classroom experiences. Just looking into the classrooms, we can see that they are no longer uniformly set up in straight rows across an obvious front of the room—with the teacher in position there. Many are, but not all, and differences within one school are common. The variety of how lessons are taught is substantially greater, and the attention paid to diverse cultures is widespread. The surface reflects evidence of deeper change that pervades the whole of classroom teaching. All of which reflect the efforts of the entire cast of educators who have been involved in researching, theorizing, planning, and teaching since the middle of the twentieth cen-

tury. There are always troublesome gaps between the efforts of educators who are working at one level of involvement and another
at any given time, but when the long view is taken, it is possible to
be encouraged by the quality of education that is now available to
many more students than is typically believed—more students
than not. Just as Cremin (1961) demonstrated that Dewey's influence was assimilated without the progressive label, so it is now for
the humanistic pressures that have emerged since. In the minds
of educators, individual children's needs have risen in importance.

The second kind of accomplishment is found in noticing how
humanistic teaching has developed where it is practiced more deliberately. Schooling is recognized as a complex interwoven community with pressures from a variety of stakeholders, more today
than in the past, that requires often-painful compromises. But
with this understanding comes less polarization than that which
surrounded the progressive education movement and the radical
changes of the 1960s. A variety of factors contribute to this more
practical and nuanced way that humanistic goals are achieved.
There is a willingness to satisfy students' deeply rooted images of
what school is supposed to be by combining what is humanistic
with what is traditionally more familiar—from which stems a helpful balance. There is a common commitment for finding the creative means for better meeting children's needs. And without striving to fulfill a grand agreement, it is possible to achieve a better
sense of being on the same page with other teachers who know
that this is of utmost importance. Joining in, the academic community offers more support than ever, because professors are
more in touch with the realities of everyday schooling. We find systematic self-study (Loughran, 2006), a heightened emphasis on
caring (Noddings, 2005), and the development of a personal vision
of oneself as a teacher (Hammerness, 2006) entered among the
higher priorities. Teachers who know best about humanistic concerns are in a position to be concerned, whether or not they feel
empowered to act.

We are also keenly aware that the shadows are all too often deep
and dark, to the point of despair. Those on that end of the spectrum would say that schools today do not promise much hope for
education. Schools have been co-opted by political and economic
agendas, where it is imagined that testing will motivate children
and teachers and bring with it a brave new world. Instead, all of
the emphasis on testing creates a hostile learning environment
that destroys a sense of safety and any real challenge for students
to become passionate thinking citizens who look forward to the adventure of their lives ahead. Courage from many sides is available,

but first Donna needs to rant—just to clear her mind for a better vision up ahead. Rants don't generally call to action, but they are necessary at times to make room for hope.

DONNA'S RANT

Throughout this book, Jerry and I have applauded the small moves that teachers make to improve classrooms and school programs that have been designed by non-educators for their own political and economic purposes. As much as I support each and every one of those teachers, I know, as they do, that it is not enough. We need to do so much more to make education meaningful and relevant for all our children. It may be poetic to say that no two snowflakes are alike, but it is hard fact that no two people are exactly alike. How can it be that we allow schools to design programs in which each and every student is supposed to learn exactly the same thing in the same way as every other student? There is no doubt in my mind that we as teachers have the responsibility to provide every child with the basic learning that we know will be necessary for her or him to survive in the world, but it is also our duty to provide it in the ways, the many different ways, that children learn. Our schools are not allowing the wonderful people who chose to become teachers the time, resources, and support to really attend to each and every child. They are required to teach kindergarteners who have not yet learned to talk about their own experiences how to read about experiences that have no meaning to them. They are required to prepare children for tests of information that may or may not be important for them. And worst of all they are put in the position of giving tests, which tell their students that as people, some are better than others. Don't tell me about life letting them know that. They learn that life lesson from the start. School should be the safe place where they learn that in fact how they are as people is just fine; the place where their teachers believe they can learn what they need to know to become a valuable part of a democratic community where their opinions and efforts are critical to the well-being of the community as a whole.

One of the teaching stories that stays with me is about a youngster who had the hardest time learning to read. He struggled so. He was the best sketch artist in the school from the time he was five and if you wanted a perfect representation of something, he was the one to do it. Also, he was very good at math. What he learned in school was that even though he struggled with reading, he was a valuable person. And he learned that you might have to struggle to do what you want. This young man went on to become a high school science teacher with a master's degree from a fine university. I imagine he is helping his students struggle to get what they want. Had he taken the standardized test that is now given, he would have been a failure.

It bemuses me that in America we do not support our children in being critical, questioning, doubting students. We expect them to be docile and do as they are told. If our founders had been successful public school students, we would be singing "God Save the Queen." How do we imagine that we will have a lively, vibrant America if we do not have lively, vibrant schools full of people learning to think for themselves, question ideas, and negotiate solutions to problems? I fully realize that far too many of our students are critical and negative, but we call them the "bad kids" rather than harnessing that energy and educating it in positive, challenging ways. We lose this potential to the streets where we become rightfully fearful of it and them. Imagine what it would be like if every one of those street-smart kids were using his or her energy in positive ways, because they had been provided with educations that utilized that "smart" instead of marginalizing it. One of the most ironic and infuriating outcomes is that the teachers are blamed for these failures. It is like giving someone a feather to pound in a nail and then criticizing them for failing. We need to give our teachers the resources and opportunity to educate our children. Instead we have teachers who are burned out and counting the days to retirement. You wonder why?

Often I find myself discussing humanistic education with parents who are afraid that this will mean their child will be allowed to do just anything she or he wants without any concern for the needs and wisdom of the adults. Perhaps in the very early days of progressive education there were some places where such foolishness occurred. To us, it is clear that the folks who started schools like that did not understand what Dewey was saying. It makes no sense to even imagine that responsible adult teachers would structure such an environment. The humanistic principles that we embody in our teaching have regard for all the stakeholders and recognize that there will be constant struggles to find a balance between needs and wants. Never in all the years of teaching did I say to a child to do what you want without regard for the other children, the time, the situation, and me. But I did encourage children to choose what best served them within a structure that I felt was safe, healthy, lively and educational for them. The polarization of allowing choice without boundaries or having a rigid authoritarian environment is foolish.

I am not afraid to use the word humanistic when I talk about how I teach, though many are. For us the word means that we care about people before we care about ideas or things. Both of us thank God daily that we have had the opportunity to be part of an educational movement that values above all the teaching of the young.

ACADEMIC HOPE

Wittingly and unwittingly, the educational academic community has in the last fifty years moved from having little involvement in the practical, daily life of the classroom to active support for humanizing the enterprise of schooling. The contrast between then and now is transparent, where the methods of inquiry once required laboratories, not messy classrooms—and the findings aimed at proving theories of learning instead of understanding the many factors that contribute to students' learning and teachers' work as a whole. These factors in different guises and their interactions have always been around; however, thinking that it is essential to investigate them closely for the complexity therein is refreshingly new. Joel Spring (2005) showed how major stakeholders have risen and fallen in the balance of powers, from long before the turn of the twentieth century, and so with perspective, we can see that this is a normal course of history. In his words, religion, nationalism, pluralism, the economy, welfare, meritocracy, unions, civil rights, multiculturalism, and other sundry tags take turns in becoming the more figural pressure. Humanistic ideals sometimes get a turn on their own, or within the aims of another factor. Most recently we deplore, politics is having its turn. As Spring (p. 461) pointed out, the federal government has successfully regulated "the school curriculum to ensure that a single culture would dominate the schools," yet in view of other developments, he hopefully pondered whether "environmental education [would] be the coming moral force in public schools" (p. 472). Within this historical context, academics can be seen as enthusiastically supporting the more humanistic endeavors of students and teachers, those that support being in charge of doing their own job.

The pattern is similar for Larry Cuban (2003, pp. 54–55): Worried mostly about the American public school becoming an arm of the economy, he too pressed for a healthier diversity, because "educational orthodoxy is bad for American schools." In a kind of rant, while not emotional in its scholarly dress, he forcefully argued that a worthy education must coincide with the aims of a democracy, respond to the diverse needs of children, and not place "the entire burden for achieving success on the individual student and the school while ignoring structural inequalities." For him, there has to be room for schools that represent a range of goals and methods. However, each must answer to the people who are directly involved. Whether traditional or progressive, and staying close to economic concerns as a choice is not ruled out, the essence of a democratic education requires establishing criteria that empower parents, staff, and students. They have to be focused on the goals that a school sets for itself, the development of democratic behaviors, values, and attitudes, and tellingly, the satisfaction of parents, staff, and students. True to his argument, he offered "these reflections as testimony to the wisdom of practice [his own] that each of us can extract from our practitioner experiences as we muddle through the inescapable conflicts that arise from our work" (p. 64). This implies that a good school should not be judged by a distant administration that knows little or nothing of the people who are being judged, but by those who are in a position to leaven evaluation with caring. We would only add that to learn about living and working within a democracy, the structures and the adults have to model actions that demonstrate their aims.

There is also a living history that we experience over time. It is happening in the contexts where we are interacting with our colleagues. The largest gathering we attend is the annual meetings of the American Educational Research Association (AERA) with over ten thousand participants. The conference can only be characterized as marginally focused on humanistic issues. But for those who have been attending since the 1950s, the differences in what happens at the conference are palpably moving in this direction. Qualitative research is more figural than traditional modes of investigation. Presidential speeches by and large are based on inquiries that search for meaning, not proof, that can be found in the interpretive analysis of data. Though many of hundreds of sessions are little more than listening to prepared papers, it is no surprise to be invited to interact with presenters, sit down in small groups to discuss a paper after a short introduction, or even discover that the presentation has been translated into a performance—where some form of the arts is used to convey the value of the research. The ambience overall feels like there is a spirit of adventure that welcomes everyone to become engaged; the visions that are shared are so often aimed at empowering educators and students, not controlling them. There is less hubris and much more sensitivity to the needs of students and teachers. The meetings are no utopia, far from it, but these elements are part of a fabric that embraces humanism, even if only marginally. The feeling is not marginal, but one of in-clusiveness. Nor are these changes superficial. They mirror the shifts that have taken place in the concerns of the research itself.

Some of the same benchmarks appear in overarching texts that have been published by AERA since 2000. They too reflect how academic research has evolved over the years—not wholesale humanistic programs, but its influence is telling. For example, we find in the *Handbook of Research on Teaching* (Richardson, 2001) substantial discussion of student needs, teacher differences, and social learning. Teachers are instructed to attend to cultural diversity as a major factor in how the curriculum is planned and implemented. Targeting idiosyncratic characteristics of students, Richardson introduces the concept of caring to educators as a worthy and necessary component for helping the learner succeed. The differing needs of teachers are considered a relevant factor. An understanding of a teacher's needs—by others *and* themselves—leads to the kind of knowledge that can be implemented in the classroom. There is a firm belief that teacher education students who are engaged in a process that includes reflection, ongoing teaching experiences, and interactive study with their colleagues and teacher educators moves them toward growth and change. Another shift that has occurred places social learning as critical to pedagogy. By facilitating dialogue that is egalitarian and open-ended, teachers support individual students' sense of empowerment. The relevance of children learning from each other in small groups, only an inkling in 1950, has become central to academic understanding of what needs to happen in the classroom. And, it is not surprising to find such group activity implemented in schools at all levels. Another important example is *Studying Teacher Education: A Report of the AERA Panel on Research and Teacher Education* (Cochran-Smith and Zeichner, 2005). Based on the review of hundreds of studies, the purpose of this report was to evaluate the quality of education programs in the early 2000s. The results are varied and complex, of course, because interpretations depend on a wide range of goals. Though the results show much room for improvement, they also reflect different kinds of valuable successes that can be applied by others. Furthermore, some of these successes support the development of humanistic practices, which are applicable to both inexperienced and experienced teachers. The newer programs are not likely to view teacher education as training; they are more in tune with the complexity of schooling, which requires that educating teachers be seen as a problem of interactive learning.

No longer imagining that the knowledge and skills needed are roughly the same for everyone, the aim is to facilitate the development of personal know-how that balances the intellectual and the practical. Partly, there is greater emphasis on the practical knowledge that builds up in conjunction with a variety of field experiences. More help comes from the discussion of examples that represent and problematize the experience of others. Not infrequently the evaluation of students' progress on their way to becoming teachers is based on portfolios where they collect artifacts from their studies, which allow for the creative expression of their personal learning. Together, these approaches better answer individual differences in teachers' strengths and style.

When it comes to having a noticeable impact, it's essential to include the work of Lee Shulman. *The Wisdom of Practice* (2004) gathers together insightful papers and speeches spanning his long career that add considerably to the understanding of what it means to become a good teacher. How educators think and practice today has in many ways changed as a result of the research carried out by him and the many colleagues with whom he has collaborated. Though some of this research seems diametrically opposed to humanistic concerns, a closer look reveals how he has successfully influenced a more balanced context, both theoretical and practical, of education worldwide. At the University of Chicago, Lee and Jerry worked together closely while completing their dissertations. However, after they graduated, their emerging research goals sent them off in different directions. While Jerry set off to develop the means to better realize humanistic goals, Lee pursued the dynamics of intellectual learning. Even so, ongoing dialogues from that time on have been a boon to our thinking. They have enriched the conceptual framework within which our inquiry has taken place.

As a starting point, Shulman noted, "We find few descriptions or analyses of teachers that give careful attention not only to the management of students in classrooms, but also to the management of *ideas*" (p. 219). From this simple beginning, there blossomed a body of research on the pedagogy of content knowledge (PCK), which addressed itself to the troublesome gap between knowing a subject and knowing enough about how to teach it well. Teachers must plan their lessons based on the strengths of the students in a class, how subjects can be uniquely transformed into a compelling set of challenges, and made easier or more difficult as a situation requires. For him, pedagogical content knowledge is what most likely will distinguish "the content specialist from . . . the pedagogue" (p. 228). Because we have not focused as much on the intellectual side of learning, his research fills out the gap. Wherever teachers are making efforts to be more humanistic, they must not lose sight of the nature of each subject in order to succeed in teaching it well. To this we have added the recognition that integrated learning built into challenging projects, like publishing the *P.L. Paper*, facilitates the process of learning in unusually dynamic ways.

As significant as PCK, a deepened understanding of the wisdom of practice is an equally important contribution resulting from Shulman's scholarship. We appreciate this work, because it explains how practice, together with the insights of more traditional research and the experience of others, becomes the primary source of information for improving practice. This view, in our minds, is connected with the extensive research that he in collaboration with Judy Shulman, his wife, have carried out on the use of cases that document the experiences of others and transform them into powerful tools for learning about teaching. Dialogue focused on experience is the key and serves as a model for reflecting on one's own experience. In this way, practice precedes theory. Shulman observes how it is generally believed that theories are to be put into practice, but "I, on the other hand, am the kind of person who finds things that work in practice, and then I try to make them work in theory" (p. 505). This is an apt description of the majority of our research.

Finally, Shulman must be credited for the emphasis on the value of researchers, teachers, and students becoming an integral part of learning communities. Together, Lee and Jerry learned this at its root in classes at Chicago with Schwab in the undergraduate college and in the Department of Education. Highlighting the value of learning as a social process, Shulman expands the notion of professional development as a forum for academics and teachers to learn together and from each other. Significantly, he advocates that teachers should have adequate power over their domain: "Teachers must understand the grounds for the competing demands on their time, energy, and commitment. They must be free to make choices that will cumulate justly in the interests of their students, the society, and humanity. Moreover, they need the opportunities to influence policy as well as respond, to initiate as well as broker" (p. 157). He believes, in our words, that teachers be treated humanistically. Our priority is to privilege the needs of students; his privileging the needs of teachers is a model for what is entailed when taking either course of action.

THE WORD

What it means to be a teacher varies with conceptual and practical understandings of the job to be done. With the infinite interactions between the two views, the wise course of action is a process open to change as experience is gathered. So it is when one desires to be a humanistic teacher. There are many facets to consider— including those we have discussed, and those are still evolving in our minds. And oddly, whether to use the word *humanistic* or not is a decision that has to be made. It's intriguing that in some textbooks the problem is discussed and in others ignored.

Obstacles arise when people voice objection to humanistic practices because they fear humanistic practices will corrupt students. We all know of strong concerns that religious faith will be undermined; there are other concerns about children not learning enough. What best supports learning is of issue, but curiously, the objections can be finessed when *humanistic practices* are not named as such. Two introductory education texts, quite similar in how many of the same topics are presented, take an opposite position.

Lynda Fielstein and Patricia Phelps (2001) include a section boldly entitled, "Humanism." It is presented as one of a range of philosophies from which students can choose to guide their teaching or to combine with others in an eclectic approach of their own making. The tenor of Fielstein and Phelps's text reflects the value of Rogers's concepts of realness, acceptance, and empathy, and they go on to highlight attention to student needs, the significance of choice, and mutual respect that comes from encouraging students to voice their opinions and ideas without fear of judgment. Following this discussion, Fielstein and Phelps give an example, point to limitations, and offer some advice. After telling of a teacher who thought she was teaching humanistically by offering excessive choices irrespective of appropriateness and then complaining that her class was in total chaos, they comment, "Teachers should use reason and moderation when applying humanistic practices" (p. 53). Fair enough. But they add, "Do not sacrifice students' success to quibble over semantics. Nothing stops you from behaving humanistically toward others—just don't call it that" (p. 54).

The second text, by Kevin Ryan and James Cooper (2001), labels a discussion of a similar set of concepts under the title *progressivism*. It too is an oftentimes no-no, but maybe a little less, because it doesn't so neatly invoke secular humanism as a threat to religious education. Ryan and Cooper view teachers as choosing a philosophy or creating an eclectic one, and add that using eclecticism should not be "an excuse for sloppy thinking" (p. 349). With progressive education in mind, they highlight Dewey instead of Rogers, but the discussion as a whole overlaps considerably with Fielstein and Phelps. Their goal is "to make the schools more humanistic" (p. 337). Consistent with our starting point that students' needs come first, they note, "Progressive educators believe that the place to begin an education is with the student rather than with the subject matter" (p. 338). However, when it comes to naming, they see the educator taking a strong stand. They suggest that he or she would say, "I'm a progressive educator and proud of it. I'm not ducking that label just because it is unpopular in many quarters these days, usually among people who don't really understand what it is. Quite honestly, for the life of me, I cannot understand how a teacher can be anything *but* a progressive educator" (p. 338, italics in the original).

Using the word *humanistic* is not a moral issue in our eyes. But it does make a difference. The choice to be a humanistic educator places *compromise* and *taking a stand* at odds. Both are viable. For us, choosing what to name what we do represents leadership. Humanistic education is unique; it entails a learning environment that offers children something special. Join the community or don't, but recognize the commitments that are involved. We appreciate there are other paths that can be taken that will similarly benefit students greatly. Where one is starting from is the determining factor, and what realistically can be expected to yield success has to be gauged. Fear that inhibits doing anything is sure to be debilitating. Risking, as a model for students, is the least we can offer them, since this is exactly what we expect of them when challenged to learn what they don't know.

In the middle ground, where no bad names are attached, a good place to begin is with *Developing a Pedagogy of Teacher Education* (Loughran, 2006). The work starts with teacher educators developing a pedagogy that is integrally connected with self-study and moves on to inviting their education students to do the same. The underlying assumption is that our vast experience as students has much to teach us about being a good teacher. Teacher educators and their students alike are asked to critically examine their practice, and each other, with the express purpose of motivating themselves to be responsible for their own learning. Willingly then, they will come to understand that doing so is messier and riskier than neater ways of becoming a teacher. The payoff is to receive a more realistic and lively education.

To reach their goals, teachers have "to be sensitive to releasing control in order to manage the complexity of teaching . . . to depart from their well-marked path and approach *the edge of chaos* in order to re-embrace the creativity, experimentation and risk-taking that so shapes a developing understanding of pedagogy" (Loughran, 2006, p. 35, italics in original). Educators are expected to model self-change to preservice teachers, who are expected in turn to model this to the children in their classrooms. In every case, it is a student-focused approach, not an educator directed one, that leads to open questions, an interest in students' views and thinking, withholding judgment and accepting a range of responses, flexibility about time, and attention to sharing the purpose and reasons for doing learning tasks (see Loughran, 2006, p. 83). For both teachers and students, Loughran emphasizes relationship, sensitivity, trust, honesty, and independence. They too are expected to be both philosophical and practical.

Originating a central concept of caring, Nel Noddings (2005) developed a comparable humanistic approach to teaching and learning that calls attention to the emotional climate. Self-study emphasizes a learning process; here, the starting point is a learning environment that is established to undergird the whole of schooling. Conceived as larger than the responsibility of each teacher alone, the concept calls upon schools to build communities in which students feel a sense of belonging, what she calls a continuity of place and people. Amidst the severe alienation that students can experience, from lack of attention to tragic events, there has to be evidence that efforts are being taken to change. In some measure, students have to be "aware that their schools are conceived as centers of care—places where they are cared for and will be encouraged to care deeply for themselves" (p. 65). This for Noddings reflects a primary purpose that promotes students' engagement in their education.

Making a learning environment based on caring work means keeping in mind the challenge of interpersonal connections when the teacher-student relation is intrinsically unequal. Noddings (2005) increases our understanding of the intertwining pressures that are involved. Trust emanates out of ongoing experiences where students feel it is essential. Part of this is asking students to care for other humans, other beings, and the quality of their material environment. And when this environment is working, students can then learn to care about responding to their teachers' efforts. Though unequal, relationship still means two-way interaction. She further argues that the problem extends to differences in children who are unequal in another sense, when "caring teachers listen and respond differentially to their students" (p. 19). The traditional notion of fairness doesn't hold. She sees that all children want to learn; "it is a question of what they want to learn" (p. 19). For all the theorizing, Noddings's discussion of the ethic of care comes with its own built-in caveat: "The living other is more important than any theory" (p. xix). Again, the essence of humanistic teaching is that people come before ideas.

Whatever approach is taken, a vision best guides everyday teaching. Hammerness (2006) offers a concept of vision that privileges and asks teachers to create their own. Working with teachers, she asks them to write about their ideal classroom, the roles that they and their students play in the imagined classroom, what the students are learning, and the relationship between what is happening in the mind's eye and the kind of society they want to see in the coming future. What comes out is sometimes not very humanistic, but interestingly, the process itself fits the ideal we are striving toward. In the advice that is offered for creating and developing a vision, emphasis on the subject has to be balanced with the needs of the students. There has to be an integration of intellectual and emotional concerns. And, there have to be comparisons between *what is* with what is *envisioned* to guide the improvement of practice—a proposal that is the basis of self-study. Where teacher education embraces humanistic practices or where a teacher is moving in this direction on her or his own, this view of envisioning is optimal. Visions can indeed be limiting or expanding, but on the positive side, they always unfold a space where work on oneself can begin. Effectiveness begins here.

Tensions are exposed that reveal to teachers what Whitehead (1993) called "living contradictions." Why are they important? Because they can lead one to productive change. For Hammerness, "Many people are drawn into teaching because they see it as a noble profession, and they have powerful visions regarding what they hope to accomplish." Soon, though, they find themselves lowering their expectations. "But by examining their visions and expanding their visions to address both subject matter and students, teachers can find ways to balance where they want students to go with where students are. . . . Navigating this tension is no easy matter, but it lies at the heart of their efforts to improve their practice and to sustain themselves and their passion for teaching" (2006, p. 7). In effect, Hammerness develops the concept of living contradictions, thereby giving it the means to effect change that can maintain and even heighten expectations.

THE NEED TO ACT

Some twenty years ago, we came across a quote from Thomas Merton that directed young monks how to think and behave when taking social action. Don't, he said, look for the consequences of your actions. Know in your heart and mind what you believe you need to do. Do it, and keep on doing according to your intuitions as they change. It was good advice, for it was around this time we were traveling to the Soviet Union (see Chapter 6) as part of a delegation of humanistic psychologists and educators to meet with our Soviet counterparts. Beyond our professional objectives, we were also serving as second-tier diplomats. We, like so many people at the time, were doing our small part to establish peaceful relations between East and West. Seemingly so inadequate, even though there were many such delegations, we comforted ourselves with Merton's "practical" stance. We've long since lost the quote, but the sentiment stays with us.

A large part of evaluating impact involves not worrying about it. Judging more than fifty years of teaching and research, our work together has added up. This is rewarding, but we don't forget how the better relations between East and West came with its own set of untoward consequences. Similarly, meaningful developments in humanistic practices haven't decreased the difficulties that abound in the educational contexts in which they appear. The complexity of the problems can overshadow any sense of progress. But with perspective, we can see the value, the great value, of a parallel context in which we do our daily work. Teaching can be difficult, more difficult, and so difficult that a sense of failure can pervade. Quitting at times is the only realistic alternative. Yet, so many teachers persevere in the constant hope of the joy that comes from managing to connect with and enliven students with knowledge. This passion is the key (even if difficulty is the norm). We welcome ourselves to life, the life of a teacher, and keep as focused as we can on what's working well. Teachers we have met with from all over the world have in them a call to be humanistic to some degree. There are small pockets of people who create genuinely humanistic educational environments. We remember. We know that it is the teachers themselves who for the most part hold the humanistic vision. This is the teacher's job, see it or not.

Many have written about this kinder, but obstacle-filled, approach to education. Frank McCourt (2005) in *Teacher Man* tells of the passion amidst stories that chronicle the touching difficulties, which he knows so well how to write. Parker Palmer (1998) in *The Courage to Teach* enriches our intellectual, emotional, and spiritual life so that we might more easily persevere. Tom Poetter (2006) in *The Education of Sam Sanders* arouses our imagination in a novel about bravery—of brave people, particularly a charming fourth-grade student and his tough school principal who turns out to have another side—all in a world where it is forbidden to use books in the classroom. These are three books that we remember well, two popular and one almost unknown, among many others, that help to keep the passion alive. What they tell us is daunting, not insurmountable, yet encouraging, sometimes inspiring. They make clear that acting authentically can at the least take extra time. We may have to give up old habits. This may leave us unfamiliar and uncomfortable with how we have chosen to think, feel, and act. We risk facing failure. More likely, success is the outcome of the authenticity.

Humanistic education, humanistic practices, and those unnamed but like them, come in varied forms, and so does impact. There is the long perspective, there is at times a sense of impact in the shorter run. But influencing change is also in the air, always, guided by teachers and their creative practices, the authors of the endless books that are published, and the readers who are taken with what they learn and take the time to pass the word along.

V

Everyday

What is most real is what we do individually and collaboratively in the classroom everyday. It is not global impact but local actions that count most in our lives. Counting, however, has a double meaning. The first is about how the whole enterprise of teaching and learning becomes meaningful. This is knowable; the teacher and the students know when they feel satisfied with their efforts. The other meaning involves judging success by observations and measurements that lie outside of our internal senses. And, here is when complications set in. Too close a look at our progress turns into an overly judgmental learning environment. To learn best, we need an environment that is for the most part supportive to the teachers and students. There need be no loss of challenge, but this is in a context where strengths are the main focus for feedback. What is optimal are shared expectations, daily work together to meet them, and a small world in which there is acceptance of quandaries as the temporary end result.

In this last chapter, we explore Donna's teaching as a source of inner conflicts that she must learn to resolve. These conflicts have arisen in her leadership role at the Project Learn staff development meetings. Her expectations as a leader and those of the staff did not match. No surprise, the needs of the teachers, reflecting in important ways the current needs of the parents, have changed over thirty-five years. The process required her to change, as well as the staff, and their efforts so far have been encouraging. Mainly we are left with many quandaries that make up the real, daily substance of humanistic teaching.

- In what way do the quandaries we discuss overlap with your own?
- After reading this book, what do you see now as your realistic expectations? Add some unrealistic ones you still hope could be accomplished with some work and luck.
- What are two or three small changes you would hope to implement some time soon?
- Who might you have in mind that you wish could benefit from a humanistic teacher?

10

Local Action

Judging the consequences of local actions requires careful attention in the immediate now. The consequences of the work of an educator have to be evaluated, and they require attention to a multiplicity of expectations. These expectations are imposed by and on teachers, students, and everyone else who gets involved. Learning has to be evaluated, social behavior all too often has to be moderated, and the source of expectations and the interactions between them all draw together a complex picture. What ensue are divergences of expectations that must be considered, because they may skew the context. Divergent expectations among people means working at odds with each other, which hardly gives an accurate assessment of possibilities. There is no clarity without an awareness and understanding of how divergent expectations have impinged on the outcomes.

EXPECTATIONS AND QUANDARIES

Whether or not teachers are aware of these dynamics, they are for the most part looking for students to share their expectations. The same is true for what students want of their teachers. Teachers want enthusiasm for the subject and a willingness to work hard, without interference in classroom interactions, while students want appreciation for whatever they contribute and a teacher who understands and takes into account their life circumstances, large and small. This is a kind of meta-expectation that underlies our many discussions of meeting student needs. Success in finding and creating shared expectations is what makes for a learning environment in which it is the easiest to teach and to learn efficiently, effectively, and with the best chance of giving individuals the attention they expect. There are times when a teacher might do better to impose as few expectations as possible, moments when students blossom given as much leeway as possible. There are other times when way too many expectations have accrued. Maybe it is supposed that by having a full set of explicit expectations everybody will get in line. Expecting too much, by teachers or students, often leads to disappointment.

Most classrooms meet enough teacher and student needs, even when significant disappointments and questions of expectations stay outside of awareness. In spite of budding problems, a class can function within reasonable limits. The differences that exist may rankle some, but they aren't causing significant disruptions. In this climate, sufficient trust has been built to assure at least some creative teaching and a show of learning. But it is also a time when heightening awareness might be propitious. Certainly, early signs of disruption are a signal to stop the normal process and get to work on underlying dynamics.

When divergent expectations start to cause real problems, it's not too late, usually just the time for more work. And now, there is no functional choice but to get the expectations out in the open. Once on the surface, they can be analyzed. Trust is the major factor. Maybe the teacher simply doesn't trust herself or himself to ask for what is really wanted of the students. Maybe the students feel too cowed and therefore unwilling to express expectations that imply criticism or disappointment. Or, students may be acting out, criticizing the teacher, without saying what is really bothering them underneath it all. There may be a mismatch about the level of limits or challenge that is operating. This is when a discussion of the class process is due (or long overdue). It can be scary for a teacher to consider authority as something that is open for discussion. But when tensions already exist, it might be a good time to better think them through. In an environment where awareness has been heightened, we have a chance to figure out where these expectations could be modified so as to improve the situation for everyone. It's hard to believe that a productive discussion of expectations can occur. Faith in the process, trust in each other, a sense of humor, maybe some fun, all are in order. Yes, it's a tall order.

Whatever the dynamics of divergent expectations, a teacher would do best to be a little flexible. Sometimes, for a class or for an individual, there might be close to none, some (as usual), or way too many expectations. None means no more than those required to hold the social fabric together. Some means those special ones that help to clarify the challenge that is intended. Too many is what gets in the way of finding shared expectations.

Usually the divergence is sensed between people, most often between the teacher and the students. Oddly, the compromises that have been made one at a time in good faith, when taken as a whole midway through some crisis, can feel like having sold out. Yet, another kind of divergence is surprisingly hidden within the self. We all have conflicting feelings and thoughts to some degree. These conflicts can be the cause of a loss of sureness and confidence, what we think of as agency. Making ourselves aware of them puts us in touch with conflicting goals, masked disappointments, and a lack of trust in the process. Yet again, some divergent expectations arise from conflicts between other stakeholders. Certainly, this happens frequently among teachers and parents, and as well emerges as a source of tension between children and parents. For us, we wonder about our notions of education and how well they will fit with Dylan and the expectations held by our daughter Rachel and son-in-law, Eric. Aunt Simone's expectations, like those of an Aunty Mame for Dylan, figure in too. And, this can become a divergence of expectations within the family.

Even if conflicts are not intractable, the feelings are often close to despair. Finding a solution to this quandary may appear impossible. The tasks are likely to be overly demanding, maybe saddening or uncomfortably iffy, for sure time-consuming, and maybe a lot of things all at once. Deciding what to do is unlikely to be best guided by logic; it is really a matter of intuition. Still, knowing enough to keep intuitions intelligent and heartfelt makes the tasks probably doable. There is a cultural norm, except for those who are satisfied with spiritual enlightenment, that requires speed in deliberation and sureness of answers. Yet, a bit of the spiritual energy does help us to move more slowly, and with this perspective, there comes a humility that allows us to accept a world filled with quandaries. It is the daily facing of these quandaries, not speed and answers, that ultimately can make an education lively for all and effective. Judging local actions under these circumstances comes closer to the truth, or at least, closer to a reality one wants to expect.

INNER CONFLICT

Jerry: The summer of 2004 Donna attended the Herstmonceux Castle Conference on Self-Study of Teacher Education Practices in East Sussex, England, where she presented a paper entitled, "What

Happens to the Self in Self-Study?" This was the fifth of these conferences that had their beginning in 1996. Following the presentation, the community discussed the kinds of intrapersonal change
that can result from self-study research. Working with the idea that
our selves are multidimensional, the discussion covered a wide
range of insights that were least of all intellectual, and most of all related to emotional growth. The focus of the discussion was a response to an inner conflict of Donna's that had been explored in her
paper. Emerging feelings highlighted connections with the act of
teaching, the process of doing research, interactions with the participants in the research process, and the effects on other areas of life.

From a more typical academic view, the topic of the discussion
centered on self-studies that ranged from little interest in self to
those that were essentially defined as forms of self-analysis. Many
studies are primarily aimed at the improvement of practice, not as
opportunities for personal growth in the realm of teaching and
teacher research. The question posed in the title reflects this distinction. The contention of the paper, however, is that whatever
choices are made by an investigator in setting up a study, there are
effects on the psyche that are well worth investigating. To wit, the
study Donna made of herself in the role of a facilitator for staff-
development meetings with the teachers at Project Learn two years
prior. Since retiring from teaching, now mainly occupied as a psychotherapist, she was in a good position to examine her own motives, feelings, ego, fears, and interests in relation to this role—
knowing of course that it is never easy. Rethinking the practical,
original goals of staff development, she took on the task of probing
her relationship with the teachers and how it affected the outcomes
of their work together.

The research began in 2002 as part of working for a year with
the teachers of Project Learn to study the structure, time, and organization of afternoon group meetings ("Group") that have long
been an integral part of the curriculum (see Chapter 4). The time
for Group had been established in the program from the very start.
Consistent with an adherence to Dewey's philosophy of education,
the mission of Group was to foster cooperative learning, integrated
studies, affective learning, democratic practices, and humanistic
interactions among the students and the teachers. The school day
was divided between morning and afternoon: The day began with
reading and math classes, assigned according to children's abilities and needs, and an assortment of classes in science, art, and
other disciplines as electives from which to choose. The age range
could be quite wide in any class. In the afternoons, the children
were grouped closer in age; together they designed a course of

study that integrated a range of disciplines, which required the students as a group to complete a project that might take several weeks or much longer to accomplish.

Since Donna stepped down, the time allotted to Group had been drastically reduced, and its purpose radically altered. There had been increasing pressure from parents to include many more subjects in the curriculum. Time for these subjects was taken from the afternoon program. At this point, Group for many children more accurately resembled the traditional homeroom. New teachers who had joined the staff initially questioned the whole idea of the afternoon program as it once was, and some of the veterans were mostly satisfied with the status quo. What softened the teachers' defensive position were some questions posed by Donna in connection with a related study (Allender, 2002): Who is responsible for students' learning? What is the role of the teacher? And, how is it different from the role of the students? The discussion of these questions seemed to renew their interest in Group; at least, they were motivated to think about what it might take to reinstitute some of the original intentions of the afternoon program. Donna reported on a few of the projects that were particularly successful. The initial discussions turned out to be encouraging, but major roadblocks were still in place.

A commitment was made to spend one staff meeting a month for two years focused on the structure and content of Group time. This was faithfully carried out each month in the 2002–2003 school year. The first meetings covered a history including the structure. Each teacher then shared how she or he was now spending the time allotted to Group, and this was followed by filling out a questionnaire that led to discussing descriptions of what they would ideally like to happen. They pondered how much time they would like to set aside each week for these activities. At the end of the first year, several teachers reported how helpful the process had already been so far. Changes in the design of their existing groupwork had been made, including small allotments of time for doing cooperative projects. The expectation was to continue the next year; a main objective was to ascertain what they were willing to give up in the curriculum to make Group more like it had been in the past. Overlapping this expectation, Donna sensed that she and the staff had some fundamentally different goals.

Unexpectantly, disappointment and anger were in store. A community commitment to participate in an evaluation process necessary for school accreditation led to postponing the meetings for an entire year. More staff time was needed than originally planned. Donna was asked as well to help with the evaluation process. First, there was disappointment. But then, the pause allowed room to look more closely at her feelings and what underlay her motives for doing staff development in connection with Group. She became aware of strong feelings concerning the outcome of her work with the teachers. Anger came up. She realized that efforts to iron out compromises with the teachers had lacked sincerity. Her less than authentic patience with the few who she felt were undermining the discussion transformed into fuel for the subdued anger. She had become not just critical but disheartened by the present state of Group in the school.

It was time for self-study. Though the stated goal was to figure out a new structure that the teachers felt suitable for the school at present, her expectation was to readopt the design developed in 1970. With this awareness, she understood that she was not interested in real change. Only returning to what she conceived of as a philosophically sound program would satisfy her. From the foundation of her education as a therapist, she remembered what Perls, Hefferline, and Goodman wrote (1951, p. 438): "The inhibition of self, in neurosis, is said to be an inability to conceive of the situation, as changing or otherwise; neurosis is a fixation on the unchanging past. This is true, but the function of self is more than the accepting of possibilities . . . it is to differentiate between 'obsolete responses' and the unique new behavior called for."

It was not as if Donna had become a neurotic person, but there was no question that her behavior, less than functional, was well described. The task was to help the staff attain their goals, and she wanted it done her way. Neither fully open to the process nor truly respectful of the people with whom she was working, it was she who first had to change. The question of motives was now in the forefront. Stephen Mitchell (2002), an analyst, discussed the problem of the changing self in relationship with others. Interaction and outcomes are a function of how one approaches oneself and the purpose of the interaction. Donna writes,

> Though it appeared that I was consulting with the staff in a lively, interactive way, I needed to become better aware of the purposes, and choices, involved in doing this work. How were my purposes affecting the work? I had to clarify what it was I wanted. I know that as an educational consultant, it is important that the teachers' needs are met. I was there to help them find the most effective way to use Group time. But with whose goals in mind? I expect myself to be a good consultant. But I also wanted the staff to accept and affirm the original design of Group at Project Learn. I had to acknowledge why this is so important to me. I discovered that not only did I believe the original design was educationally sound, I wanted the staff to accept it for personal reasons. I wanted affirmation as an educational leader and visionary. I

wanted to be important to the present staff. Underlying these feelings was the need to be right (Allender, 2004, p. 18).

As it were, Mitchell (2002, p. 109) countered, "What becomes of self-knowledge in this view? Is it healthy to be deluded about my own importance? My place in the universe? My significance to others? Of course not. What is healthy is the capacity to sustain multiple estimations of oneself, different ones for different purposes. In this view, an inability to recognize one's shortcomings can be an obstacle to meaningful, mutual exchanges with others."

Having meaningful, mutual exchanges with the members of the staff was important to Donna. Having a say in the outcomes was also important. The outcome of the work should be a joint and collaborative effort, the product of discussion, disagreement, dialogue, disappointment, and ultimately creative, healthy confluence. "Healthy confluence" was the rub; it so often doesn't happen this way (Perls et al., 1951). It was now apparent to her that in the first year together, she really wanted the staff's confluence, which was to be achieved by taking in her ideas whole without careful evaluation. Confluence achieved in this way—what is called introjection—necessitates the loss of self. There is little room for conflict or disagreement. She did not want the teachers to pick apart the design, incorporating only those parts that made sense to them. As to Donna, the confluence represented her loss of self as well. As a Gestalt therapist, she knew this happens due to isolation or focus on the maintenance of equilibrium. Direct conflict and interpersonal contact is what heightens self. The fear of rejection of any part of the whole kept her from making real contact. After self-study, she moved closer to appreciating the differences that had become unknowable (Latner, 1986). There was a willingness now to allow for the differences.

A memorable metaphor that Mitchell (2002) offers is the sandcastle. All significant relationships require joining in the building of them. As children on the beach know, sandcastles are bound to wash away. This is not cause for complete despair. Yes, there is loss, hurt, and all that goes with it. But, if there is time, new castles can be built and relationships renewed. The metaphor is a sign of hope. Donna concludes,

By exploring my previously unacknowledged motives and needs, I opened myself to change and the possibility of lively, interactive decision-making. By using this awareness in future interactions with the Project Learn staff, our work will better allow for an exploration of both our conflicting ideas and where we agree. Ideally, this will bring us to a creative confluence that does not require a loss of self but the coming together of self and other. Doing this, "the privacy of our isolated self is gone; instead we allow another to share our experience, to know us" (Latner, 1986, p. 57). Ideally, we will build a valuable, new design for Group that shows growth on my part since 1970. (Allender, 2004, p. 18)

The study in the long run clarified how Donna's inner conflict had been hidden in the turmoil of interacting with the teachers, in changes in the school's curriculum that had occurred under new leadership, and in subtler changes that had taken place in additive increments over time—some beginning even before her retirement. This larger perspective stemmed from reflections since then. Donna reflects on this in the next section in her own voice.

PROJECT LEARN: AN EVOLVING SCHOOL

Project Learn functions like a living organism that has continued to change over the years. It remains a wonderful school for children, families, and teachers. Yet, I feel conflicted about many of the changes that have transpired since I retired in 1992. What is my issue? It may be resistance to change, but more likely it is a sense that there are humanistic teachers in a fragile not fully humanistic educational program. In some ways, the classrooms at Project Learn are becoming similar to those at the Summerhill School, where the teaching resembled traditional English classrooms. I struggle with the discrepancy between my vision of Project Learn and what it is today. And, I know clearly that the direction of the school belongs to the parents and mostly to the teachers who design and implement the program. I am a grandmother, no longer one of the mothers of the school.

The school of today reflects much of the original intent with regard to how children are taught. The core values were hammered out and written down in 1970 by the teachers with help from Jerry. We wanted the school to develop a sense of responsibility for one's own learning and behavior. Students should be encouraged to define both their own meaning and meaning in common with others. The values included gaining knowledge and developing thinking, emotional, and physical skills. Evolution occurred as the values were expanded and amended at town meetings over the years. However, some of these changes impacted on the meaning of the core values in critical ways. They changed the day-to-day life of the students.

Many more subjects are now seen as essential to success than in 1970. At that time, the parents had faith that children would learn how to learn, though they did insist on required classes in reading and math even then. Now there are demands for computer classes, language classes, history, and science classes. Earlier those subjects would have been integrated into studies of topics that were especially interesting to and chosen by the students with their teacher. Now they are taught as discrete subjects. With the increase of what is considered required by the adult community, there is a serious reduction of how much responsibility and choice students have for their own learning. To the extent that they are all expected to study the same things and learn the same material, they are not being regarded as separate individuals with unique needs. Time will tell how this shift in parent concerns affects the basic nature of the educational program. If the staff could help parents become less frightened about the future of their children, they will again be able to trust their children's ability to struggle to find more of their own way in the learning process. This shift also influences the number of cross-age classes being offered. There is much less time for classes that involve fourth grade students with junior high students so that this very important way of learning has been diminished. And, the social learning from working together has been reduced. There has been a significant loss of integrated learning opportunities for the older students of the school by the reduction of time allowed for Group. It was during those times that students learned to interconnect science, art, music, math, and social studies in solving problems and presenting information to themselves and others.

In effect, the community is saying it trusts the adults to participate in the democratic process with the assurance that each person will be regarded and get her or his needs met. Yet, this same trust is not extended to the students thus limiting their sense of responsibility for their own learning and their own commitment to a really democratic process. There is no question that PL students have many experiences in working out problems using consensus, actually many more than young people in most other schools. And, it was never intended that students would make all the decisions, but it was essential to its humanistic program that they could find their choices among the possibilities presented by their teachers. As the possibilities continue to be reduced, the chance of slipping into a much more traditional educational program becomes highly likely.

The core values and customs that have survived intact are not to be disregarded. There are no tests that compare children; there are no letter grades given at any time. The consensus process though inefficient and time-consuming is valued and used for reaching all community decisions. There is no principal; this is equally inefficient and often confusing. There is equality among the staff, which shares the work of a principal. All the staff members make the same salary. Hiring and firing are done by a committee of parents and teachers who choose to be on the committee with everyone in the community welcome. Students are accepted on a first come first served basis. It's a community willing to struggle with how this vision can best be expressed.

Best of all, Project Learn has survived with a sense of vision intact. My conflicting feelings were somewhat soothed recently after attending a daylong parent/teacher retreat. What was clear by the end of the day was that the staff and parents are as deeply concerned about the core values of the school as any group ever was. Ideas were evaluated in light of the values and the desire to keep the school an essentially humanistic environment. Participants spoke and listened respectfully yet were able to challenge each other as well. They worked on the serious issue of whether to give scholarships for achieving greater diversity in the school. After a day's work, there was a consensus with everyone heard and regarded. Scholarships at this time will not be available to the families of new students, but there will be money to keep families in the community. This distinction honored the belief that no family should be admitted to PL on the good will of someone else, and it acknowledged the commitment of the community to support members in need. This is not the end of the discussion. The democratic process, which is essential to a humanistic environment, is clearly in place.

Attending graduations of eighth graders affirms my conviction that PL remains an educational light in Philadelphia. It is the custom of the school that every graduate and her or his family speak at the ceremony, not only the parents and siblings, but maybe a grandparent or a loving neighbor (even I have been asked to speak). All the people who are committed to that student have an opportunity to express their feelings. Though it may often turn into a long process, it is a moving one. Last year, Jerry, Fran Fox, and I sat together overwhelmed by what was said about how our school had been such a gift to each child. As well as caring for and making a safe place for children, they all remarked how PL empowered students to negotiate their needs in the world. Parents regularly commented on how their child has grown as a socially conscious human being. What a tribute to a school!

Some of the values developed in the 1970s are in conflict because of changing times. In the early years, the tuition was kept very low by keeping the teachers' salaries unusually low. In 1971, when the town meeting decided to raise the teachers' salaries by $1,000 to $6,000, Fran came in the next morning and said the tuition was too high and the salary increase had to be cut. The staff called a new town meeting, and the salary and tuition were lowered. The truth was that the teachers at that time, both the men and the women, were married to people who could support their families. During the 1980s things changed. Single people and single parents were hired as teachers, and it became necessary to increase the salaries. With salary increases came higher tuition and less economic and racial diversity in the community. Because Project Learn philosophically did not have a scholarship program, many new families who wanted their children to attend PL chose schools where they would get financial assistance. This changed the racial balance and economic diversity of the school. In the past few years there has been an effort to rebalance the make-up of the school.

When I walk through the school, I see engaged children. It is messy and lively with ample evidence of interesting activities. And the artwork is stunning and everywhere. Yet, too often there are classes where a teacher is standing in front of a group of students who are sitting and attending. I am caught between excitement and disappointment. I know Project Learn is, as David Winnicott said about mothers being good enough, "a good enough school." But I am not sure that is enough for me . . . though it may have to be.

A LETTER FOR DYLAN
(AND HIS TEACHERS) FROM DONNA

In the last of this series of letters, Donna writes personally of her hopes for Dylan's education. What we have written up until now has been about our education, how we think about teaching and learning, and some of the things we have done to bring them to life. Here, her interest and concern are about how our thinking and experiences might apply to his life.

Dear Dylan,

Soon, you'll be in kindergarten. Wow! I hope you will be going to Project Learn. But of course, your mom and dad are the ones who will decide. No surprise, though, if you pipe up with your own opinion on the matter. Over the years, more and more say about your education will be yours.

For nearly two years, Grangran and I have been thinking and writing about what it means to be a humanistic teacher. We've worked at making it clear why it is so vital to us for children to be educated in this way. All the while, we have thought deeply about what we want and hope for you as you grow and learn. But whether or not you are attending Project Learn, we hope at least that your school is enough like Project Learn to get the kind of education we think is so important.

What comes to mind first are my dear friends Fran and Nancy, who started the school together with me. We were committed to the idea that children come first before we even met. More than this, the three of us always checked in with each other about whether one of our "great ideas" was just that or whether it served the interest of every child. We kept each other honest, and we had each other's backs. I hope you have such teachers. They have to be willing to try out new ways of teaching when dissatisfied with their first attempts—setting a model for you, so that you learn to be willing to risk trying new ways of learning, because you like the challenge. In this way, you find out that you are the person responsible for your learning and that teachers trust you to take good care of yourself and learn what you need and want to learn (though Nancy always makes sure you are neat about it).

It would be good too if your teachers had been prepared by teacher educators who know about self-study, like the ones with whom we work. They could be John or Tom, because these two know that they have to model how they teach for their students. With this model, these young men and women who are just starting out in their classrooms are more likely to be honest with themselves. This helps them to be lively, interested facilitators of your learning. Or, if someone like Stefinee were part of their teacher education, your teachers would probably use humor and have faith in people to learn how they need to learn. You would have space to try, to fail, and to learn from your mistakes. What comes out is often something new and unexpected.

Altogether, your school should be a community of families who learn together and work together for the well being of all. I hope you are in a place where the people have a high priority on the value of both caring and challenge. Not only should your teachers care about you, they should emphasize how important it is to your life to care about your friends, your family, and the whole community of humans on this planet. Your great-grandfather, Abe Sclarow, used to tell me that we need to care for our neighbors all over the world for very selfish reasons. He would say that the germs don't know if we are rich or poor. If our neighbor gets sick, we can get sick. So we must take care that they don't. I don't really think he was selfish at all. He wanted me to know I have a responsibility to my community, and I want your schooling to help you learn that.

A science teacher like Mr. Trump, who taught me chemistry in high school, is necessary too. In his class, the magic of learning and the mysteries of discovery became clear. And, it was fun too. He took the time to make it happen. Not everything was covered in the standard curriculum. But instead of covering everything, he pointed us toward many different resources and amazed us with finding out things on our own. Perhaps you'll learn to use old books or new books, to do research on your own or with a group, to interview people who have the knowledge you seek, or to just sit and think about what it is that interests and puzzles you.

I want your education to be messy. When children are trying things out and changing their minds and looking for new ways, it is messy (not always neat). When teachers are planning curriculum to capture the liveliness of every child in the class, it is messy. When children are allowed to make mistakes and try again and talk to their classmates about what might work and to help each other solve problems, it is messy (and noisy too). And, I want you to know that you will clean up at the end of the day for it is there that you learn to clean up the environment as you live in it.

Of course I would also like you to know the plays of Shakespeare. Your great grandmother, Bessie Sclarow, gave me a book of his complete works when I was twelve years old. You may not love Shakespeare as I do and that is just fine, but I want you to love something that touches you to create and express yourself in unforeseen ways. For me, reading science fiction has opened my ways of thinking and knowing the world I live in. But beware of humanistic teachers. They can get pushy like any other teacher. You need a school where you can say, no, this is not meaningful to me.

Well, in a nutshell, I wish for you more than a humanistic teacher. Grangran and I wish for you a whole humanistic education. And more again, I hope that you will stand on my shoulders, and those of your parents, and see much farther than I. I do love you very much.

In peace, Nana

References

Allender, D. (2002). Just who is responsible for my learning? In C. Kosnik, A. Freese, and A. Samaras (Eds.), *Making a difference in teacher education through self-study*. The Proceedings of the Fourth International Conference on Self-Study of Teacher Education Practices, Herstmonceux Castle, East Sussex, England (pp. 11–14). Toronto, Ontario: OISE, University of Toronto.

Allender, D. (2004). What happens to the self in self-study? In D. L. Tidwell, L. M. Fitzgerald, and M. L. Heston, *Journeys of hope: Risking self-study in a diverse world*. The Proceedings of the Fifth International Conference on Self-Study of Teacher Education Practices, Herstmonceux Castle, East Sussex, England (pp. 17–19). Cedar Rapids, IA: University of Northern Iowa.

Allender, D. S., and Allender, J. S. (1971). *I am the mayor: Inquiry materials for the study of city government*. Philadelphia: Center for the Study of Federalism, Temple University.

Allender, J. S. (1982). Affective education. In H. E. Mitzel, J. H. Best, and P. Rabinowitz (Eds.), *Encyclopedia of educational research* (5th ed.) (pp. 94–103). New York: Free Press.

Allender, J. S. (1986). Educational research: A personal and social process. *Review of educational research, 56*(2), 173–193.

Allender, J. S. (1991). *Imagery in teaching and learning: An autobiography of research in four world views*. New York: Praeger.

Allender, J. S. (2001). *Teacher self: The practice of humanistic education*. Lanham, MD: Rowman and Littlefield.

Allender, J. S. (2004). Humanistic research in self-study: A history of transformation. In J. J. Loughran, M. L. Hamilton, V. K. LaBoskey, and T. Russell (Eds.), *International handbook of self-study of teaching and teacher education practices* (pp. 483–515). Dordrecht: Kluwer Academic Publishers.

Allender, J. S. (2005). The practical and scholarly value of the self-study of teaching and teacher education practices. In F. Bodone (Ed.), *What difference does research make and for whom?* (pp. 93–107). New York: Peter Lang.

Ashton-Warner, S. (1963). *Teacher.* New York: Bantam Books.

Bettelheim, B. (1950). *Love is not enough: The treatment of emotionally disturbed children.* New York: Collier Books.

Bloom, B. S. (Ed.) (1956). *Cognitive domain. Handbook I of taxonomy of educational objectives.* New York: David McKay.

Bodone, F. (Ed.) (2005). *What difference does research make and for whom?* New York: Peter Lang.

Brown, G. I. (1971). *Human teaching for human learning: An introduction to confluent education.* New York: Viking.

Bruner, J. S. (1962). *On knowing: Essays for the left hand.* New York: Atheneum.

Bruner, J. S. (1966). *Toward a theory of instruction.* Cambridge, MA: Harvard University Press.

Bullough, R. V., Jr. (2006). Developing interdisciplinary researchers: What ever happened to the humanities in education? *Educational Researcher, 35*(8), 3–10.

Bullough, R. V., Jr., and Pinnegar, S. (2001). Guidelines for quality in autobiographical forms of self-study research. *Educational Researcher, 30*(3), 13–21.

Cochran-Smith, M., and Zeichner, K. M. (Eds.) (2005). *Studying teacher education: A report of the AERA panel on research and teacher education.* Washington, DC: American Educational Research Association, and Mahwah, NJ: Lawrence Erlbaum.

Cole, A. L., and McIntyre, M. (2001). Dance me to an understanding of teaching: A performative text. *Journal of Curriculum Theorizing, 17*(2), 43–60.

Cox, J. (1984). [Graduation statement]. *P. L. Paper. VII*(7), 4.

Craig, E. (1972). *P. S. your [sic] not listening.* New York: New American Library.

Cremin, L. A. (1961). *The transformation of the school: Progressivism in American education, 1876–1957.* New York: Vintage Books.

Cuban, L. (2003). *Why is it so hard to get good schools?* New York: Teachers College Press.

Cubberley, E. P. (1919). *Public education in the United States: A study and interpretation of American educational history.* Boston: Houghton Mifflin.

Dennison, G. (1969). *The lives of children: The story of the First Street School.* New York: Vintage Books.

Denzin, N. K., and Lincoln, Y. S. (Eds.) (1994). *Handbook of qualitative research.* Thousand Oaks, CA: Sage.

Dewey, J. (1900) (reprinted in 1990). *The school and society.* Chicago: University of Chicago Press.

Dewey, J. (1938). *Experience and education.* New York: Macmillan.

Eisner, E. W. (1991). *The enlightened eye: Qualitative inquiry and the enhancement of educational practice.* New York: Macmillan.

Elbow, P. (1986). *Embracing contraries: Explorations in learning and teaching.* New York: Oxford University Press.

Featherstone, J. (1971). *Schools where children learn.* New York: Liveright.

Feldman, A. (2003). Validity and quality in self-study. *Educational Researcher, 32*(3), 26–28.

Fielstein, L., and Phelps, P. (2001). *Introduction to teaching: Rewards and realities.* Belmont, CA: Wadsworth/Thomson Learning.

Getzels, J. W., and Jackson, P. W. (1962). *Creativity and intelligence: Explorations with gifted students.* New York: John Wiley and Sons.

Gilligan, C. (1982). *In a different voice: Psychological theory and women's development.* Cambridge, MA: Harvard University Press.

Glasser, W. (1969). *Schools without failure.* New York: Harper and Row.

Graves, F. P. (1913). *A history of education in modern times.* New York: The Macmillan Company.

Graves, F. P. (1936). *A student's history of education: Our education today in the light of its development.* New York: The Macmillan Company.

Hamilton, M. L. (Ed.) (1998). *Reconceptualizing teaching practice: Self-study in teacher education.* London: Falmer Press.

Hammerness, K. (2006). *Seeing through teachers' eyes: Professional ideals and classroom practices.* New York: Teachers College Press.

Hilgard, E. R. (1948). *Theories of learning.* New York: Appleton-Century-Crofts.

Holt, J. (1964). *How children fail.* New York: Dell.

Horten, M., and Freire, P. (1990). *We make the road by walking: Conversations on education and social change.* Philadelphia: Temple University Press.

Kohl, H. (1967). *36 Children.* New York: New American Library.

Kohl, H. (1984). *Growing minds: On becoming a teacher.* New York: Harper and Row.

Krathwohl, D. R., Bloom, B. S., and Masia, B. B. (1964). *Affective domain: Handbook II of taxonomy of educational objectives.* New York: David McKay.

Kuroyanagi, T. (1982). *Totto-chan: The little girl at the window* (D. Britton, trans.). New York: Kodansha International.

Latner, J. (1986). *The Gestalt therapy book.* Highland, NY: Gestalt Journal Press.

Lipka, R. P., and Brinthaupt, T. M. (Eds.) (1999). *The role of self in teacher development.* Albany: State University of New York Press.

Loughran, J. J. (2006). *Developing a pedagogy of teacher education: Understanding teaching and learning about teaching.* New York: Routledge.

Loughran, J. J., Hamilton, M. L., LaBoskey, V. K., and Russell, T. (Eds.) (2004). *International handbook of self-study of teaching and teacher education practices.* Dordrecht: Kluwer Academic Publishers.

Loughran, J. J., and Northfield, J. (1996). *Opening the classroom door: Teacher, researcher, learner.* London: Falmer Press.

Loughran, J. J., and Russell, T. (Eds.) (2002). *Improving teacher education practices through self-study.* New York: RoutledgeFalmer.

Manke, M. P., and Allender, J. S. (2006). Revealing the diverse self in self-study: The analysis of artifacts. In D. Tidwell and L. Fitzgerald, *Self-study and diversity* (pp. 249–265). Rotterdam: Sense Publishers.

Maslow, A. H. (1962). *Toward a psychology of being.* Princeton, NJ: D. Van Nostrand.

Maslow, A. H. (1968). *Toward a psychology of being* (2nd ed.). Princeton, NJ: D. Van Nostrand.

McCourt, F. (2005). *Teacher man: A memoir.* New York: Scribner.

Mitchell, C., and Weber, S. (2005). Just who do we think we are . . . and how do we know this? Revisioning pedagogical spaces for studying our teaching selves. In C. Mitchell, S. Weber, and K. O'Reilly-Scanlon (Eds.), *Just who do we think we are? Methodologies for autobiography and self-study in teaching* (pp. 1–9). New York: RoutledgeFalmer.

Mitchell, S. A. (2002). *Can love last? The fate of romance over time.* New York: W. W. Norton.

Mitroff, I. I., and Kilmann, R. H. (1978). *Methodological approaches to social science.* San Francisco: Jossey-Bass.

Neill, A. S. (1960). *Summerhill: A radical approach to child rearing.* New York: Hart Publishing.

Neill, A. S. (1992). *Summerhill: A new view of childhood.* New York: St. Martin's Griffin.

Noddings, N. (2005). *The challenge to care in schools: An alternative approach to education* (2nd ed.). New York: Teachers College Press.

Palmer, P. J. (1998). *The courage to teach: Exploring the inner landscape of a teacher's life.* San Francisco: Jossey-Bass.

Perls, F. S., Hefferline, R. F., and Goodman, P. (1951). *Gestalt therapy: Excitement and growth in the human personality.* New York: Bantam Books.

Petrovsky, A. V. (1985). *Studies in psychology: The collective and the individual* (F. Longman, trans.). Moscow: Progress.

Pinnegar, S. (1995). (Re)-experiencing student teaching. In T. Russell and F. Korthagen (Eds.), *Teachers who teach teachers: Reflections on teacher education* (pp. 56–67). London: Falmer Press.

Poetter, T. S. (2006). *The education of Sam Sanders.* Lanham, MD: Hamilton Books.

Reason, P., and Rowan, J. (Eds.) (1981). *Human inquiry: A sourcebook of new paradigm research.* New York: John Wiley and Sons.

Richardson, V. (Ed.) (2001). *Handbook of research on teaching* (4th ed.). Washington, DC: American Educational Research Association.

Richert, A. E. (1992). Voice and power in teaching and learning to teach. In L. Valli (Ed.), *Reflective teacher education: Cases and critiques* (pp. 187–197). Albany: State University of New York Press.

Rogers, C. R. (1951). *Client-centered therapy: Its current practice, implications, and theory.* Boston: Houghton Mifflin.

Rogers, C. R. (1969). *Freedom to learn.* Columbus, OH: Charles E. Merrill.

Rogers, C. R. (1983). *Freedom to learn for the 80's.* Columbus, OH: Charles E. Merrill.

Russell, T. (1995). Returning to the physics classroom to re-think how one learns to teach physics. In T. Russell and F. Korthagen (Eds.), *Teachers who teach teachers: Reflections on teacher education* (pp. 95–109). London: Falmer Press.

Ryan, K., and Cooper, J. M. (2001). *Those who can, teach* (9th ed.). Boston: Houghton Mifflin.

Samaras, A. P. (2002). *Self-study for teacher educators: Crafting a pedagogy for educational change.* New York: Peter Lang.

Sarbin, T. R. (1986). *Narrative psychology: The storied nature of human conduct.* New York: Praeger.

Schön, D. A. (1983). *The reflective practitioner: How professionals think in action.* New York: Basic Books.

Schön, D. A. (1987). *Educating the reflective practitioner.* San Francisco: Jossey-Bass.

Schwab, J. J. (1962). *The teaching of science as enquiry.* Cambridge, MA: Harvard University Press.

Schwab, J. J. (1969). *College curriculum and student protest.* Chicago: University of Chicago Press.

Shulman, L. S. (1986). Paradigms and research programs in the study of teaching: A contemporary perspective. In M. C. Wittrock (Ed.), *Handbook of research on teaching* (3rd ed.) (pp. 3–36). New York: Macmillan.

Shulman, L. S. (1988). Disciplines of inquiry in education: An overview. In R. M. Jaeger (Ed.), *Complementary methods for research in education* (pp. 3–17). Washington, DC: American Educational Research Association.

Shulman, L. S. (1991). Joseph Jackson Schwab, 1909–1988. In E. Shils (Ed.), *Remembering the University of Chicago: Teachers, scientists, and scholars* (pp. 452–468). Chicago: University of Chicago Press.

Shulman, L. S. (2004). *The wisdom of practice: Essays on teaching, learning, and learning to teach.* San Francisco: Jossey-Bass.

Shulman, L. S., and Keislar, E. R. (Eds.) (1966). *Learning by discovery: A critical appraisal.* Chicago: Rand McNally.

Silberman, M. L., Allender, J. S., and Yanoff, J. M. (Eds.) (1972). *The psychology of open teaching and learning: An inquiry approach.* Boston: Little, Brown.

Sparks, D., and Loucks-Horsley, S. (1990). Models of staff development. In W. R. Houston (Ed.), *Handbook of research on teacher education* (pp. 234–250).

Spring, J. (1997). *The American school, 1642–1996* (4th ed.). New York: McGraw-Hill.

Spring, J. (2005). *The American school, 1642–2004* (6th ed.). New York: McGraw-Hill.

Taylor, S. J., and Bogdan, R. (1984). *Introduction to qualitative research methods: The search for meanings* (2nd ed.). New York: John Wiley and Sons.

Thelen, H. A. (1954). *Dynamics of groups at work.* Chicago: University of Chicago Press.

Thelen, H. A. (1960). *Education and the human quest.* New York: Harper and Brothers.

Thirabutana, P. (1971). *Little things.* Godalming, Surrey, UK: Fontana/Collins.

Tidwell, D., and Fitzgerald, L. (2006). *Self-study and diversity.* Rotterdam: Sense Publishers.

Tidwell, D. (2006). Nodal moments as a context for meaning. In D. Tidwell and L. Fitzgerald, *Self-study and diversity* (pp. 267–285). Rotterdam: Sense Publishers.

Vasconcellos, J. (1987). [A tribute in memory of Carl Rogers]. *AHP Perspective*, May, p. 7.

Vygotsky, L. S. (1978). *Mind in society: The development of higher psychological processes.* Cambridge, MA: Harvard University Press.

Warner, W. L., Havighurst, R. J., and Loeb, M. B. (1944). *Who shall be educated? The challenge of unequal opportunities.* New York: Harper and Brothers.

Weber, L. (1971). *The English infant school and informal education.* Englewood Cliffs, NJ: Prentice-Hall.

Weber, S. (2005). The pedagogy of shoes: Clothing and the body in self-study. In C. Mitchell, S. Weber, and K. O'Reilly-Scanlon (Eds.), *Just who do we think we are? Methodologies for autobiography and self-study in teaching* (pp. 13–21). New York: RoutledgeFalmer.

Weber, S., and Mitchell, C. (2004). Visual artistic modes of representation for self-study. In J. J. Loughran, M. L. Hamilton, V. K. LaBoskey, and T. Russell (Eds.), *International handbook of self-study of teaching and teacher education practices* (pp. 979–1037). Dordrecht: Kluwer Academic Publishers.

Whitehead, J. (1993). *The growth of educational knowledge: Creating your own living educational theories.* Bournemouth, Dorset, UK: Hyde Publications.

Zeichner, K. (1999). The new scholarship in teacher education. *Educational Researcher, 28*(9), 4–15.

Index

About the Authors

Jerome S. Allender is a retired professor of education at Temple University. His two most recent books are *Imagery in Teaching and Learning: An Autobiography of Research in Four World Views* and *Teacher Self: The Practice of Humanistic Education.* **Donna Sclarow Allender** cofounded the Project Learn School in Philadelphia in 1970. She taught there for twenty years and is currently a member of its administrative committee. She is also a practicing psychotherapist.